# In Wisdom's Paths

# In Wisdom's Paths

*Edited by*

Barbara B. Smith & Shirley W. Thomas

**BOOKCRAFT**

SALT LAKE CITY, UTAH

Library of Congress Cataloging-in-Publication Data

In wisdom's path : insights and inspirations for LDS women over fifty / edited by Barbara B. Smith and Shirley W. Thomas.

    p. cm.

Includes bibliographical references.

ISBN 1-57345-640-3

    1. Christian women--Religious life. 2. Middle aged women--Religious life. 3. Christian women--Conduct of life. 4. Middle aged women--Conduct of life. 5. Aging--Religious aspects--Church of Jesus Christ of Latter-Day Saints. I. Smith, Barbara B. II. Thomas, Shirley W.

BV4579.5 .I5 2000

248.8'43'088283--dc21                                       99-087695

Printed in the United States of America          72082-6636

10   9   8   7   6   5   4   3   2   1

# Contents

# Preface

It isn't common to separate people into age groups after they reach about age eighteen. In fact, many people (women especially) stop telling their age about then. And now comes along a way of thinking that celebrates the whole idea of growing older. It is good, really, because in this newer mindset one can enjoy the peculiar pleasures of each age as it happens. And aging is something that happens to us. Our only real control is to like and enjoy it or resent and run from it.

Looking through current materials about aging, we discovered, with interest, that among the primary methods being suggested to help increase enjoyment of life in the later years are journal writing, keeping individual and family histories, and other things that are usual for people active in our Church. We learned that what we believe, if lived and followed, provides well for transition into the older years, another example of the wholeness of the gospel.

Our approach, then, in writing to women of age fifty and beyond is not "how is it done?" Because those we are thinking of, Latter-day Saint women, already know this, and are so busily engaged, many have not noticed they are in the "older years." Rather, our approach has been "what does it add or mean to have these extra years?" And "what have you especially enjoyed that is a product of the later years?"

To do this we have selected from the Doctrine and Covenants fourteen topics as guides to chapter content. In relating each chapter to a passage of scripture, we hope to draw upon the wisdom and goodness in the word of the Lord. Although any of the books of scripture, or any combination of them, could have done as well, we chose the Doctrine and Covenants for its latter-day focus.

The first chapter starts the book with an overall admonition regarding "Walking in all holiness before me" (D&C 21:4), recognizing that a woman's spirituality will be matured through her years of experience, resulting in her becoming not so much older as better—more sensitive, more compassionate. There follows a discussion of qualities that might be a part of holiness, and the chapter concludes with outward evidences of holiness shown in kindness to others.

Next is a turn to the physical, with "To strengthen the body and to enliven the soul" (D&C 59:19). In this chapter health and fitness are the focus, but with the positive point of view that there need be no yielding to the years. Fifty and more is certainly not a time to turn over one's life to the calendar; there is a vital segment still to be lived. We shift from ourselves to the immediate world around us with "Organize yourselves . . . establish a house" (D&C 109:8). Sometimes the changes taking place in our personal lives, such as illness or death of a spouse, can occasion the need for adjustments. We may find a shifting of responsibilities for finances, maintenance of the home and the vehicles—the estate in any sense.

There may need to be an expanding of our capabilities, an awareness of things we need to learn; withal, we need a sense of control.

Next is the charge to "Keep a history . . . of all things that transpire" (D&C 85:1). This is not a new idea to any of us, but this may be the first time we have been able to respond as we would like. We have included journal writing with the keeping of histories. These activities, more than some others we could undertake, have immediate as well as long-range value. Their worth may not be fully known for generations. "That [ye] shall be healed" (D&C 124:104) is a subject close to the heart of some, as it talks of actually freeing oneself of old hurts and unresolved wounds of the heart. It is sometimes necessary to confront these "hidden hang-ups" directly to resolve them and then enjoy full peace again. This is written by a professional person, recognizing there are sensitivities for some.

Although it is stated in an imperative form, "Ye must grow in grace and in the knowledge of the truth" (D&C 50:40) suggests the opportunity to study and learn, which can be enhanced by the freedom that may come in increasing years. Included will be gospel study, surely, but knowledge of other good things as well.

Bringing the eternities very close to us is a chapter on "Temples and the performance of ordinances therein" (D&C 138:54), with a discussion of the sacred work conducted in the temple and how it can touch a life intimately. Closely tied in purpose is the notion that "Whatsoever you bind on earth, may be bound in heaven (D&C 127:7). The powers of heaven are involved in this work, as witnessed by the marvelous, even miraculous, events that occur in the research of names.

Many women can find a fulness for their retirement years in the richness of this work.

"Remembrance from generation to generation" (D&C 127:9) is a lively topic about families, their traditions, and the bonds that hold through generations. This is a chapter that will profit anyone interested in strengthening a family. Passing a heritage from one generation to another can make more difference to individuals and families than can be measured.

"And more blessed are you because you are called of me to preach my gospel" (D&C 34:5) is a wonderful promise. For those who have long wanted to serve a mission, this chapter will be of special interest, as it is focused toward senior missionaries. Included are actual examples of the special help senior couples can be to the work.

As Latter-day Saints, we are taught to "Study and learn . . . good books . . . languages, tongues, and people" (D&C 90:15). Pursuing interests and developing talents can add joy and vitality to our lives. In addition, if we have eternal goals, these interests can also add to our usefulness in the Lord's work.

An area that we do not often hear about but that may be of special interest to some is a focus on the land: "And I have made the earth rich, and behold it is my footstool" (D&C 38:17). This chapter includes statements of many Church leaders regarding the earth on which we live. From the days of Joseph Smith there have been those who were mindful of the earth as the Lord's footstool, and of the fact that we have some responsibility for it. Speaking of the world in another sense is "Lay aside the things of this world, and seek for the things of a better" (D&C 25:10). This chapter considers what is involved in the shifting from a structured, governed, controlled-by-circumstance world to one in which a person has freedom to set her own agendas. How does one manage to include it all, to have the desired gospel focus and yet enjoy the enrichment of the good things of the world?

Our book closes with a chapter about Eve, the first of all women, the prototype: "Among the great and mighty ones . . . our glorious Mother Eve, with . . . her faithful daughters" (D&C 138:38–39). We feel a sympathy with her and sense that she may feel that with us. This chapter includes discussion of the basic nurturing responsibility given to Eve, her relationship to Adam and his responsibilities, and how these might have led to her crown of glory.

We think this is a glorious time of life for a woman. She is in a position to see evidence of the years she has lived, to appreciate the blessings she has, to see some of the fruits of her labors, to enjoy the "settled" love of family and friends. At the same time, she can look ahead to opportunities for growth, improve places in her life she would like to change, take on new challenges where she can see a chance to make a difference, and have the time to do the things she has long wanted to do with and for children, grandchildren, and special people of whatever ages. And in all this, she can deliberately, thoughtfully prepare to meet Father in Heaven and his Son.

We hope that, through the shared experiences and insights in this book, the reader will see the advantages and the peculiar joy maturity can bring to her life. We hope she will gain increased thankfulness for Jesus Christ and determination to live her later years close to him.

# Acknowledgments

While it was our privilege to set out what we could conceive this book to be, it has come about through the facilities of first Bookcraft and now Deseret Book Company. It was our great pleasure to be associated with Cory Maxwell, who as a mentor and supervisor was unfailingly considerate and helpful. He has the talent to give wise counsel that makes one feel he is extending praise. We have found working with Emily Watts, Bookcraft imprint associate director for Deseret Book, a splendid experience. She has added to the pleasure of the project and has helped so much in bringing the book together.

To think of bringing the book together is to think of the group of talented women who have written the chapters, each one a master of her art and at the same time a faithful servant of the Lord. We are deeply indebted to them and believe that you will feel this way about them also as you read the useful, inspiring material they have prepared for you. It has truly been a privilege for us to be associated with them in this endeavor. Also, critical to the beauty and integrity of each chapter is the insightful mind and skillful hand of editor

George Bickerstaff. It has been our pleasure to know him as the precise and proper gentleman who can polish a piece to make it ready for print.

To all of these, and to others who have had a part in the completion of this book but may not have been mentioned, we express deepest gratitude. And always, we acknowledge that nothing of worth comes about without the Lord's direction and blessing and truly pray it may be so with this endeavor as well.

# Rose Is a Rose Is a . . . ?

IN ANSWER TO "REMEMBER ME?"

I know that I know you . . . your name can't be lost.
Both your name and your likeness have got to be tossed
In a crevice inside my mental computer
Where lately response to my best roto rooter
Says a rose is a . . . Blast! If I only could name it!
Some swifter cognomer has somehow to claim it,
'Cause since I passed fifty, the best I can do
With a name of a something, a someplace, a who,
Is just to keep hoping that something subliminal
Fills in the blanks that are max in their minimal.

When meeting, I plead, right off, without jesting,
No wry accusations, suggesting, inquesting.
Just say who you are—even nephew or daughter—
Be more than a blotch on my over-blotched blotter.
And then should your matter start greying some too,
I promise, I'll do just the same, friend, for you.

—Emma Lou Thayne

## Chapter 1

# Walking in Holiness

**SHIRLEY W. THOMAS**

*"Walking in all holiness before me"* D&C 21:4

This book does not begin at the beginning. It starts somewhere midway in life, going to the later years. And although its province is women of age fifty and beyond, the emphasis of the book is not on years but on options, opportunities, and outcomes. It is on seeing life through, on being great "finishers" of life.

We are familiar with the expression used to describe the eager, well-prepared starter as one who "hits the ground running." We have a scriptural guide for this chapter that just as aptly describes the faithful Latter-day Saint woman who, always looking toward Zion, wants to make continuing growth and progress as long as life allows and then to finish it worthily. She is one who is "walking in all holiness before [the Lord]" (D&C 21:4).

We are not overly concerned here about the end of our lives but about what will help us stay close to Christ while we actively engage in life's pursuits. We still have much to do. It does not escape us that the Lord has chosen for his spokesman on the earth an eighty-nine-year-old prophet—one whose earlier responsibilities, as demanding as they may have been, have not excused him from further duties, but have prepared him to now speak for the Lord. Our model as women is Sister Marjorie Hinckley as we see her walking ably at the side of the prophet. While we know few will ever speak *for* the Lord, most of us long to speak *to* him in some eternal realm, and the preparation we make now will be appropriate for that meeting.

It is interesting that in this scripture the Lord does not speak of where the walk will lead but only describes the character of it, that it will be in holiness—all holiness. We hear comfort and caution in this, but especially a priority guiding us to focus first on "holiness," and "walking in" it before becoming too concerned with where we are going. Most of us have an idea of what holiness is to us, but because it will matter so much to our everlasting happiness let us look at the difference it makes.

Women in the Church's early years became acquainted with holiness through the teachings of Eliza R. Snow, long-time Relief Society leader, who related, "Paul the Apostle anciently spoke of holy women. It is the duty of each one of us to be a holy woman. We shall have elevated aims, if we are holy women. We shall feel that we are called to perform important duties. No one is exempt from them. There is no sister so isolated, and her sphere so narrow, but what she can do a great deal towards establishing the kingdom of God upon the earth."[1] We may not speak of holiness as directly now in the Church, but the counsel is as clear in regard to our developing attitudes and sensitivities and purity of heart needed to increase our spirituality. President James E. Faust told women, "You . . . are the heart and soul of any family."[2] This direction includes all women of the Church, thinking of the Church as a "family."

Holiness *is* a matter of heart and soul, of nurturing the attributes that reflect our true nature. Holiness brings us nearer to Christ, increasing our desire to be like him. When we have looked for a concise description of exactly what holiness is, we have found instead listings of good qualities and helps for becoming Christlike. President Faust continued: "[Becoming as Christ] does include building faith by testimony and example. It includes teaching the doctrines of salvation. It includes following the Savior's example of love for all mankind. It includes ministering to others." We believe holiness is all these good things; it is becoming as Christ is. The "all" in the scriptural "walking in all holiness" could also suggest that holiness includes many aspects of excellence.

In this work we have chosen to examine some of these qualities, looking when we can to see what they mean to us of fifty and more years and what our years may add to our understanding of them. Reading "walking in holiness," we wonder what "in holiness" can mean. The Savior, when praying about the Nephites, asked that "I may be in them as thou,

Father, art in me, that we may be one" (3 Nephi 19:23). Though this is not entirely the same as our circumstance, his prayer does help us to understand a little of what we want to achieve—how to be *one* with holiness.

# Faith

Looking first at faith, we "remember that without faith you can do nothing" (D&C 8:10). While providing a sense of security and settled peace, faith establishes a foundation on which to build other attributes of godliness. For example, the brother of Jared's faith was mature. At the time he was meeting with the Lord on top of Mount Shelem, the Lord asked, "Believest thou the words which I shall speak? And he answered: Yea, Lord, I know that thou speakest the truth, for thou art a God of truth, and canst not lie" (Ether 3:11–12).

Rather than believing in the words *of Christ*, the brother of Jared believed *in Christ*. He really did not have to know what the next words would be. He just knew that he believed them. He accepted Christ as the Son of God and the voice of God's truth. As we do the same, we too will know that he would only speak the truth. This is a kind of trust seldom placed in another being, but having that kind of faith in God the Father and his Son, Jesus Christ, can add immeasurable strength to the life of a woman to whom others look for strength.

Some decisions need be made only "once and for all," and there is a wisdom in knowing which these are. So much of what we confront in a day requires judgment. The words *weighing, evaluating,* and *considering* are appropriate for this. In fact, our usefulness is sometimes measured by how well we employ them. But some judgments, having been made carefully and confirmed properly, need not be reconsidered with every use. The brother of Jared knew that. It is good for us to know and to decide which judgments these are.

When we have come to this point of belief that we can trust in whatever the Lord is going to ask of us, without questioning, we have opened our lives to the powers of heaven. It does not mean life will then be trouble free, but it does mean that our Father can provide us with the particular experiences our growth requires and not just what we will accept. He can count on our assuming a responsibility for the growth of his kingdom determined by what is the need of the kingdom and not by the limitations of our willingness. It is not an ordinary kind of trust. When we sing the hymn with words by the late Elder Bruce R. McConkie, "I Believe in Christ," we may want to think of that meeting on the mountain and what the faith demonstrated there can mean to our lives (see *Hymns*, no. 134).

Another scriptural example of the effectiveness of faith relates to prayer. In this instance the faithful of the Lord among the Nephites brought a remarkable blessing to the Saints in Joseph Smith's day through their faith *in* their prayers. "And I said unto them, that it should be granted unto them according to their faith in their prayers." And also, "This is not all—their faith in their prayers was that this gospel should be made known" (D&C 10:47, 49). We could so easily read quickly over the words *faith* and *prayers* without taking note of the distinction made between faith *and* prayers and faith *in* prayers. Three times on one page the Lord makes clear that an entire people were blessed to receive the gospel because of some who not only prayed for it to be so but prayed "in faith, believing."

Having faith in our prayers seems to be as critical to the process of receiving from the Lord as the prayer itself. In the case of the lost manuscript pages of translation for the Book of Mormon, the Lord said, "Satan thinketh to overpower your testimony in this generation, that the work may not come forth in this generation." But then he explained that the work will not be thwarted: "And, behold, all the remainder of this work does contain all those parts of my gospel which my holy prophets, yea, and also my disciples, desired in their prayers should come forth unto this people. . . . And now, behold, according to their faith in their prayers will I bring this part of my gospel to the knowledge of my people" (D&C 10:33, 46, 52).

This may not be a new idea, but it may need to be renewed as a means of bringing strength to our prayers. Having faith in prayers is sometimes a matter of how much. Great faith can seem almost qualitatively different from faith with little heart.

Polynesian people are known for their extraordinary faith. On one occasion I was blessed to experience a measure of this. While flying from Tahiti to Tonga by way of Rarotonga, I realized that I could benefit from a priesthood blessing. I was traveling on a Relief Society assignment, but I had not been able to receive a blessing from my husband before leaving home, as was usual. I felt confident the back problem I experienced would respond to the medication I carried. Still I knew a blessing would be helpful. Along with me on this flight was a sister from another auxiliary organization and a Regional Representative going to the same meetings. During the trip I asked him if he would be willing to give me a blessing when we were in a suitable place. He said he would, so I waited. He mentioned nothing about it during the stop in Rarotonga.

When we arrived in Tonga there were greetings and a meeting, and then at the next break in the meetings he asked me to come to an available room. He and another priesthood holder were ready. Before the blessing, these two faithful Tongan brethren asked if I had ever received a blessing given by a Lamanite. I had not, and I wondered if I would notice something unusual—thinking of what is often mentioned about the Polynesian faith. I did feel the Spirit, and the problem responded well enough, but after I returned home I had an unusual experience of the Spirit making known to me something I could do to help solve the problem. I remembered the Regional Representative, his kindness, the time he took, and his faith.

The Lord has said in many different ways, "Whatsoever ye shall ask in faith . . . ye shall receive" (D&C 29:6; see also Matthew 7:7). But we must ask in faith. In fact, if we ask for the right things, he says, "believing that ye shall receive, behold it shall be given unto you" (3 Nephi 18:20). We may take this direction casually, but it appears that he does not.

# Knowledge

"I give unto you these sayings that you may understand and know how to worship, and know what you worship, that you may come unto the Father in my name" (D&C 93:19). Knowledge is critical to our salvation, for "it is impossible for a man to be saved in ignorance" (D&C 131:6).

This belief has colored the lives of Latter-day Saints in evident ways. From the earliest days of the Church there have been training programs for the members. Joseph Smith organized a school for training priesthood leaders that appeared in different forms intermittently until the establishment of the University of Deseret in Salt Lake City.[3]

There was also concern for the children. In 1831 W. W. Phelps was appointed, by action of the Seventies, to write some schoolbooks for the use of children, and books were to be gathered for the trip west.[4]

When they arrived in the Salt Lake Valley, many families were housed in the old fort established by the first company of pioneers, some living in wagon boxes. Even in these temporary conditions, still they held school. Zina D. H. Young, who with her small children lived for some time in her wagon box, writes of holding school for her own and other children. After she moved into "log row," where she shared two rooms with another woman and her children, a heavy rain washed the dirt roof into the rooms, covering the contents with clay and requiring a major cleanup—yet still there was school.[5] This tradition of the pursuit of learning has had an impact on the homes of Latter-day Saints to this day.

Two expressions common in our vocabulary speak of "knowing" or "knowledge," but in a way we do not usually equate with schools. One, "You should have known better," is often used as a kind of reprimand when something has gone needlessly wrong. Although the value of using this—or any— expression in the way here described is highly questionable, there is merit in giving thought to how we actually can "know better."

It has been said that the mark of the well-educated is to know the implications of one's beliefs. There is a quick and easy way to test ourselves on this, and it can be learned on the streets of New York City. My husband and I lived in that city during his graduate training and had the opportunity to work with children in two quite different settings. We, along with other Latter-day Saint student couples, worked as live-in house parents in a home for homeless children. The children were placed here because their homes were unsuitable. During the day I taught in a private school for children of the well-to-do. There were few similarities in the two groups of children, but there was one memorable thing they had in common: When presented with a statement of fact, almost to a student they would reply, "So?" This seems impertinent, but it was rarely intended to be, even in the home (and never at the school). By interpretation, it stands for "So what does that mean to me?"

This is the question we can each ask ourselves of every new fact we need to learn. As we do this and answer in a serious and conscientious way, we will begin to know the implications of our beliefs—we will "know better."

The other expression is the response a child gives when asked how well he or she knows a favorite story: "I know it by heart!" Little children know by heart the stories they have been read over and over, usually by a beloved family member or a dear friend, or they know by heart a story told many times by someone who loves the story and who no doubt loves them as well. There is a great deal of love involved in knowing by heart.

In a slightly different way, we believe learning by heart can apply even to grown-ups as we allow caring and compassion to have a place in our lives. When we have something new to learn, we can "run it past" our hearts. So often we hear, "I'll need to run that past my wife [or the boss or whomever]."

Let us consider how many places there are for expressions of the heart. Think what a revolution could take place in your corner of the world if just because of you there were a new component of caring being felt, unasked for, maybe undeserved, surely unexpected. Whether you are learning or teaching, writing or reading, try doing it by heart.

## *Humility*

"Man is nothing, which thing I never had supposed" (Moses 1:10). Of all Christlike attributes, humility is one of the easiest to grasp, probably because it is taught over and over through experience. It also may be one of the most difficult qualities to make a consistent part of our lives. It is easy to put it on, but then it slips off. It is the quality that seems to run most directly counter to the world in which we live.

The daughter of President Harold B. Lee and her family lived next door to us for a time. Our daughter, who was near in age to theirs, was occasionally at their home when President Lee dropped by for a visit. Once after such a time, I was dusting her desk and came upon this useful note she had made: "President Lee said, the most important principle of the gospel to you is the one that is the hardest for you to live." It takes little thought to understand why this is so. It would be much less painful to follow an easier way—concentrate on the ones you do well and spend less time on the more tiresome, difficult ones. But our holiness is only as pure as its least refined component.

Anytime is a good time to step back and look objectively at ourselves, but it is especially good when we yet have opportunity to make course corrections. We all understand that perfection is a work that continues into eternity. But now, while we are in the midst of life, is a good time to evaluate and consider things we may have been neglecting.

Humility may not be a difficult quality for all, but one kind of humility many of us may overlook is the need to make whatever we have seem adequate. My husband often told our children about how his home, as he was growing up, seemed grossly inadequate. For many years it served as a central meeting place for members of the Church in the isolated coastal area of southern Oregon where they lived. Often his family and the missionaries were the only ones to attend the meetings they held, but when the missionaries did find investigators, they brought them. On those occasions, even if it were two weeks in a row, his mother related the Joseph Smith story to the group. She told it with such excitement and conviction that, at least for those few moments, the investigators were riveted to what she was saying and were enthralled with the message. My husband said he heard that story over and over again countless times during his boyhood and was just as excited as the investigators to hear his mother tell it.

Their mother didn't live to see her boys mature. She never had the lovely home that she would have liked and to which she would rather have invited others, but each of her sons has treasured the testimony of Joseph Smith and the restored gospel she taught them as she taught the investigators in their modest home. They each cherish the memory of their mother and the excitement with which she made the gospel a living truth to them while at the same time minimizing the importance of the things they did not have.

# *Obedience*

"The Lord requireth the heart and a willing mind; and the willing and obedient shall eat the good of the land" (D&C 64:34). Even if we knew all the attributes that could be a part of holiness, we would not have room to discuss them fully, but surely we should include obedience. All of us who have been in the Church very long have by this time found our positive response to the membership expectations concerning the principles and ordinances of the gospel. While continuing faithful to these, we can further enrich our response.

Consider the Savior's urging to do "the works which ye have seen me do" (3 Nephi 27:21). His work most often recorded was healing the sick and teaching the gospel. It may be hard, as a woman, to actually "heal the sick" because of the need for priesthood blessings. But there are opportunities for attending to the *needs* of the sick. Many of us will care for a companion or other loved one stricken with a serious illness. Such service answers the Savior's call. It brings his love into the home and a comfort to soften the heartache of failing health. I don't know how Shakespeare knew this, but he expressed well a definition of mercy in *The Merchant of Venice* (IV, i, 184), that it is "twice blessed." Not only does it help those cared for, but the one caring in turn receives blessings. Her soul is tempered and her vision enlarged.

When loved ones are incapable of returning the love shown them, we see more clearly that we have not been loving them because they loved us in return. The teaching about Heavenly Father's love, "We love him, because he first loved us" (1 John 4:19), is not describing a trade relationship—"you love me and I'll love you." It is teaching discipleship—because the Father first loved me, and thereby taught me what love is, I can love him and his children. Caring for loved ones, even when they do not show appreciation for that caring (and maybe especially when they *cannot)*, gives us a blessed opportunity to express the love we learn from the Father. He loves us, and we in turn want to represent his love in the world. "As he *is,* so *are we* in this world" (1 John 4:17; emphasis added). "For God is love" (1 John 4:8).

Another work, teaching the gospel, may be one for which many women are especially suited at this age and time, particularly those who have grandchildren or others who fill that role in their lives. There are so many settings in which a good gospel story can be told, and in this phase of her life a woman may find time for personal study of gospel topics that can be particularly interesting to children and families. Special outings, family nights, and reunions arranged with this in mind can be the means of bringing happiness and strength and a bond that will last through time into eternity. Although doing these things may be a matter of obedience, it also holds the prospect of great joy.

## *Compassion*

"Be ye all of one mind, having compassion one of another" (1 Peter 3:8). I believe it is in reading of the Savior's acts of compassion that we can understand the pure love of Christ. Although the account of the rich young ruler, for example, is found in Matthew and Luke, reading it in Mark, where mention is made of Christ's love, I understood it differently: "He answered and said unto him, Master, all these have I observed from my youth. *Then Jesus beholding him loved him,* and said unto him, One thing thou lackest . . ." (Mark 10:20–21; emphasis added). The express statement of Christ's love for the young man makes a different story of it. The element of love changes everything. Undoubtedly this is so with our lives; people feel closer to us when we show compassion.

We are given other examples, such as when Jesus learned of the death of John the Baptist. He went alone into the wilderness, but people seeing followed him. By the time he got to the place, there was a large gathering of them. Although he really came there to be alone with his feelings, he had compassion on the people and, setting aside his needs, fed them (see Matthew 14:13–23). How many times have we been besieged by requests from others when we thought we were in need of time to ourselves? I feel immense love, honor, and gratitude for the Savior, but in reading of his acts of compassion I also feel greatly drawn to him. I am sure others have had some of these feelings. This is a lesson about people, and something to remember about one's own relationship with others.

I think of one sister who shows compassion that seems born of Christ's love. She attends the single adult activities in her ward, but not because she is in need of the social life they provide. Although she is a widow, her life is full with the association of her family and many friends. People seek her friendship. She goes to single adult functions because she knows the program needs her. She knows that by going to their meetings she helps to make the program successful for some others who do not have other interests and would have no social activities without these. For her it is a sacrifice of time and energy. Her health is poor. But she faithfully attends for the others who have need of that blessing.

# Conclusion

We believe the attributes we have considered are some aspects of holiness. They are surely not all, but discussing these may have let us realize a sort of scrutiny that can help us in observing our own lives.

And before we are entirely finished, we would like to ask, "So?" What difference can it make to us that we have talked a bit about walking in holiness? If we can turn away from such a discussion and put our *To Do* list in the same pocket where it has always been, unchanged, or if we haven't added any new telephone numbers to our *Must Calls* of shut-ins and the lonely, then maybe it hasn't mattered. The evidence of holiness achieved will lie in deeds of kindness performed.

A few people in the world have been remembered for their extraordinary bravery and compassion. But many who daily serve in remarkable ways are not known by the world but are revered by those who are recipients of their caring. One brother, for instance, upon his release as stake president, then as a missionary, began taking the daily campus newspaper to several shut-ins in his stake. These were persons formerly identified with the local university who for health reasons were no longer able to be in touch with the campus. Of course they were grateful and delighted for this daily contact. When the stake president suffered a heart attack and stroke and was himself homebound, one of those who had been a recipient took over the "paper route." This brother delivered it as he took the daily walk prescribed as therapy for his recovering three-way heart bypass.

Another, a gifted musician—so many years of her life a sought-after soloist in operas, oratorios, and choirs, including the Tabernacle Choir—has always shared her gift freely, giving her time and talent whenever she could to those who asked. She explains this, saying she has felt her ability was given her to share with others. In recent years she has suffered physical pain. Few if any hours are pain free. She is no longer as able to give with her singing. But despite her pain, she cultivates a beautiful garden. It bears abundantly at her hand. Its produce she now gives to others as she has always given the beauty of song.

When we receive kindness from others we see God's love reflected through the lives of good people. And we do see and receive so much. For the world around us, however, the causes still are many and the kindhearted yet too few. Surely we who call ourselves Saints of the Most High, disciples of Christ, "walkers in holiness," could increase that number as we strive to achieve our aims as holy women.

President Gordon B. Hinckley, speaking at graduation to those who had completed the prescribed years of training at BYU and were now leaving to see what difference they could make in the world, told them that if there is anything that is needed in the world, it is charity and kindness. He admonished that as they found success in the world they should never forget to reach out, with love and concern, to those who "walk the unsteady and wandering path of life."[6]

And where will our holy walk lead us? The path is well defined, and it will lead us to Christ. He will come in his glory, surrounded by all his holy angels. All nations will appear before him, and this is the time the righteous will hear, "Come ye blessed of my Father, inherit the kingdom prepared for you." Among these will be they who have ministered to the hungry, the thirsty, the lonely, the naked, and the imprisoned, and though they knew it not, they had, as Christ said, ministered unto him (see Matthew 25:31–40).

# Notes

Shirley Thomas and her husband, the late Robert K. Thomas, are the parents of three children and grandparents of eleven. They have lived many years in Provo, Utah, where her husband was associated with Brigham Young University. Sister Thomas served for ten years with the Relief Society general board, five of those as counselor to Barbara B. Smith.

1. Eliza R. Snow, *Millennial Star,* 13 January 1874, pp. 18–19.
2. James E. Faust, "The Grand Key-Words for the Relief Society," *Ensign,* November 1996, p. 94.
3. See "Schools of the Prophets," in Daniel Ludlow, ed., *Encyclopedia of Mormonism,* 4 vols. (New York: Macmillan, 1992), 3:1269–70.
4. See Joseph Smith, *History of The Church of Jesus Christ of Latter-day Saints,* ed. B. H. Roberts (Salt Lake City: The Church of Jesus Christ of Latter-day Saints, 1932–51), 1:185, 276.
5. See Janet Peterson and LaRene Gaunt, *Elect Ladies* (Salt Lake City: Deseret Book, 1990), p. 52; Marilyn Higbee, "A Weary Traveler" (Provo, Utah: Brigham Young University graduate study program, 1992).
6. As reported in *Church News,* 21 August 1999.

# Chapter 2

# Body and Soul

## MARGARET W. THOMAS

*"To strengthen the body and to enliven the soul"* D&C 59:19

One thing that bothers me about aging is the way people refer to others much younger than myself as being old. They might say, "She has just turned seventy. I don't know how much she'll be able to do." They vocalize that these "old" people are not able to do many things because of their advanced age. They console family members who have lost loved ones who were just past the age of retirement as having lived a full, rich life and not having much to look forward to.

Just last winter I invited some much younger friends to go

to our cabin for a snowmobile outing in Yellowstone Park. Some of the younger adults in the party asked what I would be doing all day while they were snowmobiling. My daughter piped up and said: "Don't worry about Mom. She'll be on a snowmobile, and you'll have a hard time keeping up with her." I have ridden a snowmobile ever since they first became popular. Riding them now seems no different to me from how it was that many years ago. Just because I've aged doesn't mean that I can't do many of the things I've always enjoyed.

After living for some years in the "senior citizen" category, I can say that most of us do not feel or want to act as old as our biological ages. Still, some in society expect us to look, behave, and perform in a particular way starting in our fifties and continuing into our sixties and seventies. Some of us just surrender our physique, power, strength, and endurance to these expectations. Recent research shows that for those who do not go along with society's prejudices, there may be no middle age.

## The Longevity Revolution

As the twentieth century draws to a close, one of the life-transforming achievements is the increase in life expectancy. In just these past hundred years, life expectancy has catapulted from forty-seven years at the beginning of the century to more than seventy-seven years as we reach the end. Early on, improvements in sanitation, hygiene, and living conditions helped control the outbreaks of virulent diseases. The middle of the century ushered in the use of antibiotics, and state and local health departments began instituting childhood vaccination programs, which virtually eliminated the often fatal diseases of smallpox and polio. People are living longer. It is reported that there are more than 65,000 people older than a hundred in the United States alone. And one in eight Americans is sixty-five or older.[1] A crowd of healthy, active seniors are changing the perception of aging as they demonstrate that they can learn and contribute throughout a person's mature life.

## Use It or Lose It

We should create a plan for the future that includes the programs research has identified as being able to extend our longevity. Most of us decrease our activity as we age. We become more sedentary and convince ourselves that we cannot do what we used to do because we are getting older. Not true! We can still begin aerobic training (physical exercise designed to increase heart rate and oxygen intake) well into our seventies and see huge improvement. We may not achieve the levels of people who have exercised all their lives, because the lack of consistent exercise does take a toll. The results, however, can still be substantial.

I have always believed heartily in the saying "Use it or lose it." This refers to our minds and bodies alike. We can all see the muscle atrophy that takes place when a broken limb has been encased in a cast. The same thing happens to any muscle of the body that we cease to use in the same manner as we have done in the past. If we cease to stimulate the use of our minds, a similar thing will happen.

How many times have you wished to be eighteen again, taking back with you your wisdom, experience, knowledge and your wallet? That trip back in time was science fiction a generation ago. Today, returning to your youth can be a reality. If you are between thirty and sixty, you can crank back the time on your biological clock by a staggering amount as determined by standardized human performance tests for biological age. Between sixty and ninety big gains can still be made. What's changed? Dramatic breakthroughs in nutrition, fitness technology, and sports medicine. If the idea of dragging your body back through a time warp seems like a pretty weird idea, be assured, it really works.[2]

Proper exercise and nutrition can be important factors in how well we look, feel, and perform. We need to formulate a plan and be consistent in carrying it out.

## *Eating for Health*

Let us start with the staff of life, the food we eat. We likely have developed some poor eating habits in our lives that could be changed to help us improve our health now.

William Castelli, M.D., director of the Framingham Heart Study in Massachusetts, says: "Most people have ten favorite nutritionally terrible meals that they recycle over and over year in and year out. If they'd just pick ten new meals and fall into the habit of eating them, they could accomplish all their nutritional goals."[3]

Food can be a powerful medicine. We can lose fat, grow muscle, gain energy, and vanquish hunger through the proper selection of a balanced diet. But just what does a *balanced diet* mean? What should we eat, and exactly how much of it should we eat? The United States Department of Agriculture has created a food pyramid to be used as a guideline. It tells us how many servings of each kind of food we should eat each day.

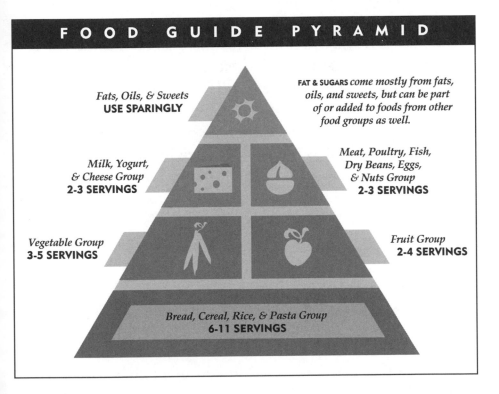

Looking at the pyramid, we can see that the largest amount of daily calories should come from grains, and the smallest amount should come from fats, oil, and sweets. In the pyramid, for example, an average serving is a slice of bread; half a cup of vegetables, fruit, or cereal; one cup of leafy raw vegetables; one cup of milk or yogurt; one and a half ounces of cheese; or two and a half to three ounces of lean cooked meat.

This pyramid puts heavy emphasis on vegetables and fruits and less on meat and dairy products. This is also the emphasis we read and study about in the Word of Wisdom. Indeed, the things of the earth were given to us by the Lord for us to use and to benefit from. In Doctrine and Covenants 59:18–19, we read: "Yea, all things which come of the earth, in the season thereof, are made for the benefit and the use of man, both to please the eye and to gladden the heart; yea, for food and for raiment, for taste and for smell, to strengthen the body and to enliven the soul."

Often, people decide to exercise and eat a balanced diet because they want to control their weight. For many people, these healthy habits do result in weight loss. As you look at the food pyramid, are you thinking, "How in the world will I be able to eat that much every day? I'd have a hard time just getting down the six to eleven servings of grain I'm supposed to eat daily!" Few of us eat the number of servings of grains, fruits, and vegetables recommended, but we certainly have no problem eating the food in the other three groups—dairy, meats, and oils and sugars. If you study your own diet carefully, you might find that you are eating close to a balanced diet and that you have room to add more grain, fruits, and vegetables.

Nutritionists also suggest we should drink eight cups of water daily (for a total of around sixty-four ounces). This does not mean fluids such as soda or fruit juices or other beverages. It means water. Water supplies much of the lubrication that is necessary for proper function of the joints, muscles, and skin. It keeps the body hydrated.

I was talking to my son Evan, an exercise physiologist who works full-time helping others improve their health lifestyles, about drinking water every day. He told me of a man in one of his programs who changed his dietary habits to include drinking eight glasses of water a day. This man had always had trouble wearing contacts. They irritated his eyes, and the ophthalmologist couldn't come up with a solution to correct the situation. After this man started drinking the eight glasses of water regularly, the trouble with his contacts disappeared. When the doctor asked what had changed, the man said the only thing he could think of was his increased water intake. The ophthalmologist started recommending drinking water to his patients, and he noticed a dramatic decrease in those who had trouble wearing their contacts.

Speaking personally, I have noticed that my skin is less dry and I feel much better when I keep up my water intake. It's a simple step toward better health. And the body quickly adjusts to the increased fluids.

Supplements like daily vitamins are helpful for some older adults who cannot get from food all the nutrients they need. Marketing in the media is doing a good job convincing people that they need expensive nutritional supplements, and claims that certain supplements can restore youthful energy and strength. Be careful. These claims can sound as if they are based on proven scientific research, but that does not mean that they are true or safe. Buyers should beware and check with their doctor before spending hard-earned money on supplements that promise results that are not needed or may even be harmful to those who have medical problems. So-called "natural" remedies may harbor salmonella or other bacteria and are often not controlled for strength or correct dosages. The best way to get the nutrients you need is through a healthy diet.

# Exercise Is the Key

In the introduction to *Exercise: A Guide from the National Institute on Aging,* Senator John Glenn states:

> You are never too old to get in shape. I am often asked what I've done over the years to stay in shape. At different times, I have engaged in many different activities. When I was in school I played football and basketball. The Marine Corps provided its own unique brand of physical training or PT. While in the space program and for many years afterwards, I jogged to stay in shape. And my wife Annie and I have enjoyed hiking and skiing over the years. Most of all, I have always valued staying active in one way or another.
>
> From my involvement with NASA, both in the Mercury program and with the Shuttle Mission STS-95, I have become keenly aware of the effect that weightlessness can have on the human body. Without the effect of gravity, astronauts' muscles and bones begin to deteriorate while they're in space. A number of other changes occur to the astronauts in orbit—from which they recover upon their return—that also happen as part of the natural aging process right here on Earth. For one, osteoporosis sets in. These same things can happen to us if we maintain a sedentary lifestyle. This is especially true as we get older.
>
> The good news is that exercise is just a step away. . . . In my case, I had to make accommodations to my advancing years by modifying my exercise regime. In the past I was an ardent jogger, but as I got older my doctor said that the impact of running was putting too much stress on my knees and other joints. He suggested that I take up speed walking instead. Along with that, I do some weight lifting and stretching. So now I still get a great workout, but by doing exercise that is appropriate for my age and physical condition.[4]

For the most part, when older people lose their ability to do things on their own, it does not happen just because they have aged. One major reason it happens is that they have become inactive. Older adults who become inactive lose ground in four areas that are important for staying healthy and independent: endurance, strength, balance, and flexibility.

Fortunately, research suggests that you can maintain or at least partly restore these four areas through exercise, through everyday physical activities. There are few reasons to keep older adults from increasing their physical activity, and "too old" and "too frail" aren't among them. The fact is that two-thirds of older adults don't engage in regular physical activity. Of course, it is always wise, especially if you have any kind of chronic disease, to check with your doctor before increasing your activity. There are many excellent sources for exercise materials. The one I have just quoted from is published by the government and is available, free of charge, for individual use by calling 1-800-222-2225 and asking for *Exercise: A Guide from the National Institute on Aging.*

As with any changes we make to improve our lives, we need to proceed wisely. We would do well to follow the instruction given by King Benjamin to the Nephites: "And see that all these things are done in wisdom and order; for it is not requisite that a man should run faster than he has strength. And again, it is expedient that he should be diligent, that thereby he might win the prize, therefore, all things must be done in order" (Mosiah 4:27).

I especially believe that we should be diligent. We need to be as diligent as the two elderly gentlemen, well into their eighties, who walk up a rather steep hill in front of my house each morning at 7:15. I could almost set my clock by their punctuality. It takes that kind of dedication to a program to achieve the desired results.

*Improve your endurance.* An endurance exercise is any activity—walking, jogging, swimming, cycling, gardening, raking—that increases your heart rate and breathing for an extended period of time. Start out slowly with as little as five minutes and gradually increase to a total of thirty minutes on most or all days of the week. These sessions can be divided into ten-minute segments.

*Improve your strength.* "Although they might not notice it as it happens, most people lose 20 to 40 percent of their muscle tissue as they get older."[5] Strength exercises can at least partly restore muscle. As a precaution, none of the exercises you select should cause pain. The range within which you move your arms and legs should never hurt. An increase in muscle that's not even visible to the eye can be all it takes to improve your ability to do things like get up from a chair or climb stairs. You should do these type of exercises two times a week. To do most of the exercises to strengthen muscle you need to lift or push weights, gradually increasing the amount of weight you use. You can buy weights from a sporting-goods store or use things like old milk jugs filled with sand or water, or socks filled with beans or rice and tied on both ends. Weights need not be expensive.

*Improve your balance.* Balance exercises are closely associated with the strengthening exercises that are used to strengthen the muscles of the lower body. These are simple exercises such as standing on one foot at a time while guarding against falling. These can be done almost anywhere at anytime.

Increasing your sense of balance can often prevent falls that are so common among the elderly.

*Improve your flexibility.* Stretching exercises will not improve your endurance or strength but are thought to help keep your body more flexible and give you more freedom of movement to do the things you need to do and the things you like to do.

## *Exercise Your Brain*

In an experiment conducted at the University of Illinois, it was found that an invigorating walk actually gives older people a good *mental* workout, boosting memory and sharpening judgment. The mental benefits of walking were especially significant, researchers said, because the senior citizens had not exercised regularly before joining the study.

As the life span of human beings is constantly lengthening, more and more elderly citizens are confronted with the problem of properly utilizing leisure time based on their desires, experience, knowledge, and abilities. In the later part of life, we have the time to pursue rewarding activities. These are the things that can "enliven our souls."

I was amazed at how much more I appreciated this wonderful world the Lord created for our enjoyment when I first took some art lessons. Although it is clear that I will never join the ranks of the Great Masters, I have learned to view a landscape in a very different way. I now see a variety of shapes with sunlight and shadows. I see colors, intense and subtle, with hundreds of shades of green in a landscape. I note clouds that are beyond description, and bodies of water with wonderful reflections that I try to duplicate in my mind as if I were to capture the beauty on my canvas. It has made the simple act of looking so overwhelmingly grand and has made me appreciate the glorious world we live in. My art has truly enlivened my soul.

One evening years ago when I was working as a nurse in the hospital, a doctor came to the desk and said, "Margaret, come here quickly." I thought that something was wrong with one of the patients, but instead he directed me into the work-room where a large window faced west. There we watched one of the most gorgeous sunsets I have ever seen, ablaze with color, a blue and pink sky, clouds outlined with glittering gold. Streaks of sunlight streamed brilliantly through it all. He said: "I just could not let you miss this. If this only happened once every twenty years, everyone would be out here to see it, but since it happens so often, no one even stops to look." The ability to see the everyday beauty around us can enliven the soul.

## Service Can Bring Joy

One of the best ways to enliven the soul is to know the joy that comes from service to others. There are so many ex-amples of service given by those who have retired from their career occupations. Today a corps of senior missionaries 4,200 strong are serving in all parts of the world as ambassadors of the gospel; in temples, Family History Centers™, and visitors' centers; in the leadership of branches and wards and mis-sions. There are those who serve in other ways when their health or other circumstances will not permit them to leave their homes.

One evening I was driving home from a ward activity with

a good friend, a sister in her nineties who told me that she had to get up at six o'clock the next morning. Surprised, I asked if she always arose that early. She said that she just had to get started early or she could never get all the things done that she had planned to do. Among the items on her agenda was to finish tatting a beautiful white handkerchief that she was going to give to a new bride in our ward. She wanted to be sure the bride could have it with her when she went through the temple for the first time. Even though this sister's physical strength was ebbing, she was still using her talents and thinking of the joy she could give to others. She also provided each new mother in our ward with a hand-crocheted baby afghan. She had to use every available minute to ensure that the blankets were finished before the babies were born.

This very special friend had lost her husband sixty years earlier and lived on a very meager income. She had no children and only a few extended family members. She was by nature rather quiet and shy, yet she had a large circle of friends, gained by her kind deeds and thoughtfulness to others. She could easily have felt sorry for herself and her circumstances and, in her loneliness, felt miserable, but instead she had a line of people at her door thanking her for her kindness to them. Even on these visits, she rarely let anyone get away without cookies or a hot pad made from her leftover yarn.

My mother, when she was physically handicapped with a terminal illness, could still bake bread and send it down the street to a less fortunate neighbor. Joy can come from many sources, but we must plan and prepare so that we can remain productive all of our lives.

I admire those who do not let advanced technology stand

in their way as they work on their family history and genealogy. It is easy to say, "I don't understand computers. I can't learn that new technology. I will have to let someone else do that for me." As I walk through the family history library, I see many proficient workers in their eighties and nineties who have mastered the computer and Internet technology to keep up with the changing programs.

When I served a mission in the Church Office Building, I saw many missionaries called to serve who had used a typewriter in the past but had never touched a computer. Some had never even learned to type, but that did not stop them from learning the skills that were required to serve in the missions to which they were called. They became masters of the computer and were ever learning and expanding their knowledge.

## Look for Ways to Serve

When I was serving as a ward Relief Society president, my husband was ill with Parkinson's disease. He was becoming physically handicapped, but he still had a very positive attitude and a desire to serve wherever he could. He asked one day how he could help me with my responsibilities. I told him of a woman who lived alone and was fearful of something happening that would prevent her from using the phone to summon help. She was afraid that no one would find her for maybe days. He immediately formulated a plan. He told me to tell her that he would call her every morning at nine o'clock, and if she did not answer, we would come over immediately to check on her. He did this for about two years. But he determined quickly that he needed to say more than just "How are you?" So he started looking up a scripture or thought for the day to share with her. She responded by doing the same thing. On one occasion she told me how much that meant to her, to spend time during the day looking up a thought to share.

A very impressive friend of mine, M. Elmer Christensen of Salt Lake City, is now in his ninety-seventh year. He has been actively involved in the Church all his life. He served a mission in Switzerland in 1925, served on the YMMIA general board for thirteen years, has been a bishop, a stake president, and one of the first Regional Representatives, and still serves as a sealer in the temple two days a week and as a stake patriarch. On his favorite old Underwood typewriter he types up the patriarchal blessings he gives. He has a large yard that he cares for, and he is proud that he daily eats the produce from his garden. His daughter reported that when his apple orchard produces abundantly, he bottles the apples into applesauce and gives the fresh applesauce to members of the family. He cannot stand to see the apples go to waste. He is always busy. He says, "It is my religion to keep busy."

Brother Christensen not only keeps himself busy physically but also is always engaged in projects where he is concerned with others. He has written his personal history, but he does not think anyone will take the time to read the 300-page volume, so he writes little mini-histories that his children and grandchildren can use for their family home evenings. He writes essays on a large variety of subjects, such as: "Why I Feel Home Teaching Is Important," "Why It Is Important to Partake of the Sacrament," and "My Feelings about Those Currently in Political Power." To help other family members become better acquainted, he also prepares short biographies of new grand- or great-grandchildren who have just joined the family by marriage. He has compiled twenty family home evening manuals he has written himself for his family members, which they all use and cherish. He sends a personal letter to each member of the family on his or her birthday, sharing some personal experience. He is also the organist for his priesthood meetings every Sunday.

Brother Christensen is blessed with good health, but most of all, he lives each moment filled with activity for both his body and his mind. As a result, he is forever young. He does not look his age. I am convinced he does not stop long enough for the aging process to get set in motion. And even at age ninety-seven, he is still making progress.

## Follow the Savior's Example

President Spencer W. Kimball wrote:

> After the Crucifixion, when the Savior was upon this continent with the Nephites and Lamanites, he said to them after days of teaching them the gospel, "Therefore, what manner of men ought ye to be?" And the answer which he himself gave was, "Even as I am." (3 Nephi 27:27.) "I, the Savior, even as I am, ye must be also. Ye must perfect your lives." He was not talking of the physical totally, and yet, that is a part of the program—that we will perfect our physical bodies. We will make them just as attractive as possible. We will keep them as healthy as possible. We will keep them in the best condition so far as we can. And so, we will make them like our Lord's. But, the most important thing is to gear our minds and our spirits so they will be like the Savior's.[6]

Those who follow the Savior are those who have kept

themselves physically fit and actively engaged in the lives and needs of their friends. They are truly living as the Savior would have them do.

President Ezra Taft Benson said:

> The most successful program of complete youth fitness ever known to man was described in fourteen words. They are the words of the beloved disciple Luke in the New Testament. He uses just one sentence to cover a period of eighteen years—the eighteen years in which the Savior of the world, after returning to Nazareth from Jerusalem, prepared Himself for His public life: "And Jesus increased in wisdom and stature, and in favour with God and man" (Luke 2:52). . . . It covers everything—physical fitness, mental fitness, social fitness, emotional fitness, and spiritual fitness.[7]

We have the model, now we should try to achieve the goal. Can we, as many experts tell us, turn back the biological clock and regain many profitable years of service and joyous living through prudent use of the resources available to us? Can we increase in wisdom and stature and in favor with God and man all the days of our lives? We can, if we follow the example set by the Master himself.

## Notes

Margaret W. Thomas graduated from the LDS Hospital School of Nursing and received her BS degree from the University of Washington in nursing education. She served as a member of the Ricks College Nursing faculty for twenty years. She served as a volunteer for LDS Social Services for twelve years, working with the adoption and unwed mother program. In the Church, she currently serves as a counselor in her ward Relief Society presidency. Margaret and her late husband, Boyd R. Thomas, are the parents of six and grandparents of fifteen.

1. See *Healthy Living for Seniors,* Regence BlueShield of Idaho, Summer 1999 issue.
2. *Dr. Bob Arnot's Guide to Turning Back the Clock* (New York: Little, Brown and Company, 1995), p. 4.
3. Ibid., p. 65.
4. *Exercise: A Guide from the National Institute on Aging,* NIH Pub. No. 98–4258, introduction.
5. Ibid., p. 36.
6. *The Teachings of Spencer W. Kimball* (Salt Lake City: Bookcraft, 1982), p. 378.
7. *The Teachings of Ezra Taft Benson* (Salt Lake City: Bookcraft, 1988), pp. 555–56.

# Chapter 3

# Establish a House

### JANET GRIFFIN LEE

*"Organize yourselves . . . establish a house" (D&C 109:8)*

How can anyone prepare for the death of a spouse? The fact that I had almost nine years' advance notice did not diminish my heartache. As the curtain closed on a lifetime with my husband, my world, as I had known it, came to an abrupt halt.

After a long battle with cancer, with several healthy years in between and even during treatments, the mortal phase of Rex's life ended. I thought I had come face to face with the trial of my faith. Or was my trial just beginning?

Struggling to establish a sense of normalcy in my shattered life, I felt out of step with everyone else's continuing on as though nothing unusual had happened. Suddenly my world seemed to have stopped, while others were moving forward. It was similar to my feeling of isolation when, as a seven-year-old, I got off at the wrong bus stop and watched the school bus leave me in a strange place. Even then, as I had to figure out what to do next, I learned some valuable lessons.

Elder Neal A. Maxwell teaches us that "customized tutorials are the extra tuition we pay for our continuing graduate education as Jesus' disciples. In discipleship, we learn of suffering that there are no exemptions, only variations."[1]

As I worked through my own "variation" of suffering, it seemed I had so much to think about, to decide, to plan, and to take care of that it was days before I could even begin to assess my new role. It felt overwhelming to be solely responsible for the physical maintenance of our house and savings, along with the spiritual and emotional safekeeping of our family. Trying to imagine what life would be like without him, I wondered, *What kind of a house will this be without Rex here?* Memories filled every room of my home, but future images escaped me. As I searched my mind and heart for answers, I turned to the scriptures, even as I sensed that I did not yet know all of the questions. But as anyone who has studied the scriptures knows, we often find our answers there, even before we have thought to ask the right questions.

My answer for the kind of house I want to have now that I am alone is the very same as when Rex was here. In the Doctrine and Covenants we find wise instruction for our organization in preparation for "every needful thing." The Lord makes no reference to our decorating styles or the challenge of single parenthood, but his simple, reassuring words, spoken with the firmness of a loving parent, suggest the structure and purpose for every house suitable for children of God. As a portion of the dedicatory prayer for the Kirtland Temple, the following scripture serves as an outline for happiness in our earthly homes while preparing us for our journey back to our heavenly home: "Organize yourselves; prepare every needful thing, and establish a house, even a house of prayer, a house of fasting, a house of faith, a house of learning, a house of glory, a house of order, a house of God" (D&C 109:8).

## Prepare Every Needful Thing

In any area of our lives, organization and preparation provide security and peace of mind. This is especially true as we confront mortality. Ideally, careful preparation should be an ongoing process.

Open communication concerning wills, insurance, investments, and trust, tax, mortgage, and banking information is invaluable. Meeting together with experts in each field is helpful and facilitates the memory of details at a time when it is hard to remember even zip codes and phone numbers. Keeping files up-to-date and accessible also helps the spouse left alone. Awareness of each other's responsibilities not only makes the transition easier for the survivor but also allows for a closer understanding between couples and simply makes good sense at any stage of marriage.

Proper attention to the preparation of wills and estate planning could mean the difference between the survivor's living comfortably or struggling economically. Estate planning is sometimes difficult to discuss while dealing with terminal illness, but if handled in a matter-of-fact way throughout marriage, it can become part of wise preparation instead of a painful task.

Family members and friends can provide loving support when dealing with funeral arrangements and other unplanned-for details. Remember that with the Lord's help, and a combination of work, patience, and the kindness of others, most problems are solvable. We are not alone; he cares about whatever concerns us. The Lord reassures us: "Look unto me in every thought; doubt not, fear not" (D&C 6:36).

Preparing every needful thing encompasses more than attention to insurance policies, wills, and funerals. Though communication about estate planning is vital, in the end it will be of only temporal significance. In contrast, preparation for eternal concerns will have eternal significance. I am grateful for the diligent planning my husband made for my temporal welfare, but I am even more appreciative of the spiritual bonds that will hold us together eternally. The memory of a good marriage and the support that comes from strong family ties, meaningful friendships, and deep spiritual roots are anchors in times of grief.

My seven children and their families are my very best friends. I delight in their growth and progress and find joy in our constant association. Frequent phone calls and visits with those who live far away, and Sunday dinners and ongoing interaction with those close by, help me continue my cherished role as mother and grandmother. To go running with my eldest granddaughter, read to a four-year-old grandson, or attend a grandchild's recital or sporting event makes my heart sing.

Friendships are eternal, I have come to understand, and

good friends continue to be good friends regardless of one's marital state. I am glad for the continuity my friends add to my life.

My spritual base has been strengthened through the experiences since my husband's death. My roots were strong, but I know I continue to grow through the process that life offers all of us.

# A House of Prayer

"Be thou humble, and the Lord thy God shall lead thee by the hand, and give thee answer to thy prayers" (D&C 112:10). How comforting these tender words have become to me! I love the visual image of being led by the hand and having my prayers answered. In the quiet moments of my life, as I think about the well-being of my family, as I recognize my own weaknesses in the shadow of my tasks, or as I ponder steps I should be taking, I bow my head in prayer. A hush comes over me, a warm feeling of stillness, a sense that someone very loving is aware of me. Often, as I think of his image, his character, and his promises, I become consumed with gratitude for our Savior, Jesus Christ, and for the dark hours he spent in Gethsemane—for me, for all of us. During these moments I feel very close to our Father in Heaven for sending his Son to redeem the world.

The first time I knelt to pray alone by the bed where Rex and I had prayed together for so many years, I was surprised to feel a familiar warmth encircle me. My anticipated loneliness was replaced with feelings of strength and reassurance, feelings of closeness to Rex and to my Heavenly Father. My thoughts centered on the sanctity of life and the similarity of spirits entering this world and leaving it. I felt grateful for a lifetime of experiences with prayer. Because it had always been a tender and meaningful means of expression, I found that even the contemplation of prayer was comforting to me at this crucial time. I didn't know where I would begin my prayer, what I would say, how I would feel, or what words to use, so I simply began to pour out my heart to my Heavenly Father.

A flow of gratitude from deep within my soul found limitless expression. I couldn't find enough words to indicate my overwhelming appreciation for all I had been given, for my husband, for our lives together, for our children, for the tender loving care we had felt during his long illness. As words formed, more thoughts came to mind.

As I concluded, a desire to repay my debt of gratitude became my focus. In complete submissiveness I asked merely to be able to serve in any way the Lord could use me. I remained kneeling for several minutes after I had finished my prayer, not wanting the warmth and comfort to leave. During the experiences of the past several hours I had felt the Spirit of the Holy Ghost and I wanted that feeling to be with me always.

Even now, when I feel alone or fearful I return to my knees, asking for guidance and comfort. Sometimes my need is in the middle of the night, and always that same sweet comfort and reassurance arrive to bless me, and I awaken in the morning with a happy heart. I have found new meaning in Alma's advice, "Counsel with the Lord in all thy doings, and he will direct thee for good; yea, when thou liest down at night lie down unto the Lord, that he may *watch over you in your sleep;* and *when thou risest in the morning let thy heart be full of thanks* unto God; and if ye do these things, ye shall be lifted up at the last day" (Alma 37:37; emphasis added).

Often, my prayerful requests are for feelings of peace, understanding of others, forgiveness, and patience. Through prayer combined with a sincere desire to receive these blessings, I have often felt a change of heart almost immediately. I am aware that our Heavenly Father knows that our first steps toward Christlike action begin with our feelings.

Although prayer may not always change our circumstances, it can change our attitude and feelings about something or someone. Elder Dallin H. Oaks teaches: "Feelings are subject to change. Our feelings are subject to our will." He continues, "My widowed mother understood that principle. 'Pray always about your feelings,' she used to say. She taught her three children to pray for the right kind of feelings about their experiences—positive or negative—and about the people they knew. If our feelings are good, we are more likely to have appropriate desires, to take right actions, and to act for the right reasons."[2]

In the midst of changes in our lives, praying for the "right kind of feelings" can help us find strength and contentment. In Philippians, Paul admonishes us to "let your requests be made known unto God. And the peace of God, which passeth all understanding, shall keep your hearts and minds through Christ Jesus. . . . Not that I speak in respect of want: for I have learned, in whatsoever state I am, therewith to be content. . . . I can do all things through Christ which strengtheneth me" (Philippians 4:6–7, 11, 13).

Answers to prayers concerning my feelings make it easier for me to exercise my agency in making righteous decisions. The Lord understands the importance of our feelings. We are instructed in Doctrine and Covenants 9:8–9, "If it is right I will cause that your bosom shall burn within you, therefore you shall feel that it is right. . . . But if it be not right you shall have no such feelings."

There are times during the process of grieving when not feeling like praying becomes a stumbling block to the progression of healing. Becoming numb to the "burning within" or the desire to pray can be immobilizing. I sometimes found myself simply praying that I might be relieved of the anesthesia of grief so that I could learn to feel and even hurt again.

Along with directing my feelings, prayer helps me organize my thoughts, prioritize my needs, and enumerate my gratitude. I have learned to tap the source of heavenly strength through prayer. Sometimes the blessings I have in mind may not be the ones I receive. My blessings might come in gaining confidence to deal with more challenges. Each time this happens, I develop renewed faith in the Lord and trust in his wisdom. I feel my Savior's love through diminished pain and alleviated fear when I cannot be given my heart's desire. Good feelings result from submissiveness to the Lord's will.

## A House of Fasting

The prophet Isaiah tells us that the Lord promises rich blessings to those who fast, that they will be free from heavy burdens and oppression (see Isaiah 58:6). If there is ever a time when we need release from heavy burdens, it is during challenges. Through my own fasting, burdens have been lifted as the absence of temporal feasting feeds my spirit. At other times, when the weight of the world seems to be on my shoulders, I have felt release, knowing others were fasting with me and carrying part of my burden. We usually fast alone and in private, but as we draw near to our Heavenly Father, feelings of loneliness disappear. The sacred process of fasting prepares us to receive the guidance and comfort we need. President Spencer W. Kimball taught: "Inspiration and spiritual guidance will come with righteousness and closeness to our Heavenly Father. To omit to do this righteous act of fasting would deprive us of these blessings."[3]

When we need spiritual strength, or when sadness consumes us, we can turn to the Lord with prayer and fasting. Fasting humbles us in preparation for our request for blessings. I appreciate the following scripture in Helaman, for the correlation it shows between fasting and prayer and the blessings of relief from unbearable sorrow. "Nevertheless they did fast and pray oft, and did wax stronger and stronger in their humility, and firmer and firmer in their faith of Christ, unto the filling their souls with joy and consolation" (Helaman 3:35).

Fasting also invites the Spirit of the Lord to be with us. When the sons of Mosiah journeyed many days in the wilderness, they "fasted much and prayed much that the Lord would grant unto them a portion of his Spirit to go with them" (Alma 17:9).

Through fasting, we confirm our ability to be obedient. As we shut out the temporal and concentrate on the spiritual, our focus changes, and we are able to more clearly prioritize, meditate, pray, and listen for answers. In giving spiritual attention to our decision process, we are able to define a righteous direction. Sometimes fasting serves to clarify things in our own minds, and we feel that our Heavenly Father trusts us to make a suitable decision from good choices. It would not be possible for me to continue in my own responsibilities with the addition of tasks that used to be my husband's without the blessings that come from fasting and prayer.

# A House of Faith

Sometimes we wish the Lord would come and tell us what to do, as he did when he instructed the brother of Jared to make holes in the tops and bottoms of the barges to get air (see Ether 2–3). But because he wants us to develop our faith, he allows us to find most answers for ourselves.

Faith is a difficult concept when we feel overwhelmed and incompetent. It helps to remember that when we have done "all we can do" (2 Nephi 25:23), we can go to the Lord, and he will make up for our deficiencies.

Many times, new challenges in our lives are accompanied by drastic changes. Sometimes our resistance to that change stifles our progression. It is hard to focus on the positive elements of our present lives without reaching backward in time, wishing for past moments, and banging on closed doors. Moving forward, adding new responsibilities and interests to familiar ones, allows for growth, stability, and faith in the future.

As I have added new responsibilities to my life, I have had to exercise great faith that my Heavenly Father would help me be equal to the task when I have felt inadequate. I know that it is through him and not my abilities alone that I have been able to accomplish many things that were beyond my capacity. I find peace in knowing he is always there.

Our faith in a loving Heavenly Father will bring us peace

if we put our trust in him. As Elder Jeffrey R. Holland has taught:

> To those who struggle to see the light and find hope, there is a promise of "good things to come." My declaration is that this is precisely what the gospel of Jesus Christ offers us, especially in times of need. . . . There *is* help. There *is* happiness. There really is light at the end of the tunnel. It is the Light of the World, The Bright and Morning Star, the "light that is endless, that can never be darkened." It is the very Son of God Himself. . . . On difficult days when heaven's help is especially needed, we would do well to remember one of the titles given the Savior . . . "an high priest of good things to come." (Heb. 8:6; 9:11)[4]

When I contemplate the faith I have in "good things to come," I think of the anticipation of new seasons, and of our participation in the preparation for each change. The miracle of regeneration moves me as convincingly in fall as it does in spring. While the earth lies dormant I marvel at the metamorphosis that will take place as winter warms into springtime and we witness the synergy between the Divine Creator and our own efforts to comply with his laws. In order to reap our individual harvest, we too must contribute effort and exercise faith.

As we look forward to "good things to come," we also connect with intangible cornerstones of our faith. They are as real as those we can touch. Our faith in gospel truth allows us to know that even though we do not recall the creation of the world, nor did we observe in mortality the Savior's birth, the Resurrection, or the restoration of the gospel, those things did happen. They were miracles performed for us. Our required participation is to obey the word of God, trusting our lives to his care.

Obedience to gospel principles brings blessings that build faith and a renewed outlook on life. When I feel discouraged, I try to become more obedient and I am always encouraged. Reading scriptures daily, attending the temple, being a little kinder to others—all these always result in a more optimistic attitude. I can look at life and be happy for the blessings of today without worrying too much about what is ahead for me.

I used to think that I wanted to know everything that was in my future. Now, I know that the burden of some things would be too great, and I am content to be happy as I exercise faith and trust in my Heavenly Father's plan.

As we are told in Doctrine and Covenants 78:17–18: "Verily, verily, I say unto you, ye are little children, and ye have not as yet understood how great blessings the Father hath in his own hands and prepared for you; and ye cannot bear all things now; nevertheless, be of good cheer, for I will lead you along. The kingdom is yours and the blessings thereof are yours, and the riches of eternity are yours."

# A House of Learning

When I was left alone to learn to do many things I had never done before, I felt a little bit like my sister who, at age six, didn't want to stop playing to learn how to tell time.

"Well, what will you do if you need to know what time it is?" our bewildered mother asked.

"Oh, I'll just ask someone who knows," was the unconcerned reply.

I was familiar with our household expenses, but I honestly didn't want to know how to manage taxes, or decide when to rotate the tires. I had been interested in our investments, but I didn't want to be responsible for them. Those were Rex's areas, and I felt about them the way he would have felt about planning a daughter's wedding.

Realizing my reluctance to take all of the burden of responsibility before it was necessary, and understanding the attention that I needed to devote to my responsibilities at BYU, to our children, our home, and the growing responsibilities of his care, Rex did three things. One, he carefully attended to estate planning. Two, he spoke with key people and explained how he thought things should be handled. And three, he found times to discuss important issues with me in as casual a manner as "final instructions to a spouse" can be talked about. For example, while shaving, he would mention, "If you outlive me, you should know that . . . ," or, while driving somewhere, "If I leave this planet before you do, I hope you will remember that . . ." We both thought that there would be time ahead when we could plan in depth.

I appreciate the constant instruction he gave me over his last few years. When the time came, I knew where things were, what I needed to do, and, just as important, I knew the people he trusted to give me advice. Some of my decisions might not be exactly what Rex would do, but I take current information coupled with good advice and make decisions that seem right. I know that he trusts my judgment and has faith in me.

My confidence has grown over the past three and a half years as I have learned new skills and become comfortable with who I am without Rex at my side. One of my greatest fears was that as I lost my role of being his wife, I wouldn't even recognize myself. I have found to my surprise that I am still the same person I have always been. However, in my new role I am finding different opportunities that were not available to me before. Learning to find a balance between the familiar and the new has helped me to be happy.

I have learned that routine and organization heal feelings of being out of control. The habit of going running early in the morning, usually with a daughter or two, has continued to help me begin each day with optimism. When I have early morning meetings, go to the temple, or attend church, I feel content with purpose and direction in other areas of my life. These things are enjoyable and fulfilling to me and therefore are helpful in the structure of my life. Some will find other ways to begin their day. The important thing is to get up and face life with eagerness, prayer, and purpose. A good start gives direction to the rest of the day.

I am constantly surprised at how happy and at peace I feel. I thought that without Rex I would no longer want to be here. To the contrary, I love life and find it fulfilling. I want to be here for my children and grandchildren as we delight in teaching each other. I have much to learn and I want to give and contribute in any way I can.

I am grateful for the gift of learning that has filled my life and replaced my desperate sadness. In the process of learning how to live without Rex, I am aware that he would want me to grow and be happy. In the book *The Once and Future King,* T. H. White retells the legend of King Arthur, who comes to the wizard Merlin sad, confused, and frustrated. Merlin advises Arthur: "The best thing for being sad is to learn something. That is the only thing that never fails. You may grow old and trembling in your anatomies . . . you may miss your only love, you may see the world around you devastated by evil lunatics. . . . There is only one thing for it then—to learn. Learn why the world wags and what wags it. That is the only thing that the mind can never exhaust, never alienate, never be tortured by, never fear or distrust, and never dream of regretting. Learning is the thing for you."[5]

President Gordon B. Hinckley points out that learning is our responsibility, saying, "There is . . . incumbent upon you, you who are members of The Church of Jesus Christ of Latter-day Saints, the responsibility to observe the commandment to continue to study and to learn."[6] I have come to understand that "the best thing for being sad *is* to learn something."

## A House of Glory

A house of glory is a house that worships God—a house that finds all things glorious that come from God, a house that reflects the grace and glory of our Savior Jesus Christ.

In his essay "The Weight of Glory," C. S. Lewis speaks of our perception of beauty, and asks what we might consider beautiful. It's not the things themselves, he suggests— whether nature, books, music, paintings—but a certain feeling these mediums trigger within us. "It was not *in* them, it only came *through* them, and what came through them was longing. These things—the beauty, the memory of our own past—are good images of what we really desire."

Lewis further states that we always have a longing to strive for our heavenly home—a kind of homesickness, so to speak. "To be at last summoned inside would be both glory and honour beyond all our merits and also the healing of that old ache."[7] I rejoice at the beauty of this earth and feel a tenderness for all the Lord has created. I long to be recognized by him as I recognize his glory.

Alma asks us, "Can ye look up to God . . . with a pure heart and clean hands? . . . Can you look up, having the image of God engraven upon your countenances?" (Alma 5:19). Even some of those who stood at Christ's feet did not fully understand who he was, but *we* can, if we *glory* in his words, his teachings, and his example, and make our home a house of glory.

I do not know how long I will remain in the house where Rex and I raised our seven children. Some days it has grown too large for me, and others it seems bursting at the seams with the laughter and playfulness of happy grandchildren. If I someday move to a smaller, calmer home, my wish is that it too will be a place of family worship where we will sing praises to our Redeemer and close our prayers in his holy name. I will hope that our thoughts and conversations will reverently reflect our understanding of his holiness and glory.

At this time in my life I find it significant to remember that even though Christ mingled with multitudes, he too had times when it was necessary to be alone—times even when he left his disciples alone. During the crowning glory of his ministry, he had to fall solely beneath all things so that he could rise above them. Alone, he had to do the work of the Father and atone for the sins of all mankind. In those long hours, the only perfect being ever to live suffered the sins of all humanity.

We know that through the sacrifice of our Savior we will be given the "peaceable things of immortal glory" (Moses 6:61). Our own loneliness, even our suffering, cannot be compared to that of our Savior, Jesus Christ, as he atoned for us all that we might have eternal life. That sacrifice, gladly offered with love and humility, is his glory (see Moses 1:39).

## A House of Order

Getting things in order after the death of a spouse is difficult. The mere presence of personal belongings brings constant reminders of a life so recently viable and interactive. The process brings bittersweet feelings of memories that seem too recent to be boxed up and put away on a shelf. Dismantling and organizing Rex's files from two offices that were moved to my garage was a long and painful undertaking. Had it not been for the comforting help of a dear friend, I would probably still be unpacking boxes and weeping.

One day, when the boxes in the garage seemed to multiply, my mailbox continued to be filled with bills, my children needed me, my car was malfunctioning, and I was trying to figure out how I would find time to attend to new Church responsibilities and speaking commitments, I felt completely overwhelmed. How would I ever organize my life? I wondered. Would I ever bring order to the chaos, and discover a comfortable rhythm to my life?

I left my boxes, got in my car, and drove to the cemetery, not because I felt closer to Rex there but because it is a beautiful, peaceful spot and I needed to get away. As I sat on the lawn by his grave I began to talk to him, pouring out my heart about my loneliness and my frustration. I began enumerating the many things I had to do and my inadequate feelings about getting it all done. The tears began to flow until soon I could no longer speak; in fact I could hardly breathe. I wished with all my heart that he could tell me what to do.

Then, as if out of nowhere, a calming feeling came. Suddenly, I knew what Rex would have said if he had been there. I smiled as I almost heard his teasing voice inside my head: "If you have so much to do, Janet, why are you sitting up here on this hill crying? Go home and get things in order and you will feel better!"

So many times I had heard Rex tell one of our children, "In the length of time it is taking to tell me why you can't get the job done, you could have been half finished!" These familiar pronouncements of logic were characteristic of my husband and the way he directed his own life. I realized I had been thinking too much about his death and my loneliness, feeling sorry for myself.

I returned home and got to work. Within minutes I came across a letter he had written to me about a year earlier in response to a fearful note I had written him. The letter began, "Janet, please do not dwell on my death. Life is good and there is so much of it yet to live."

I'm not sure how much attention I had given that letter when it was originally written, but upon my return from the cemetery that day his words touched my heart and his message to me was clear and strong. Since then I have made an effort to dwell on the goodness of life, even when I am dealing with the ongoing organization of the parts of our lives that used to be his responsibility. Without my eternal companion for the duration of my mortality, I find strength and order in living as I attempt to establish a house that will anchor me and prepare me for eternity, as well as provide a helpful balance in my daily life.

When I think of order, I also think of the temple, the quiet order there as well as the order and organization of the creation of the world and the plan of salvation. There is no disorganization in God's plan for his children. Everything has been carefully outlined and designed. The Master's plan is in place. We need only to follow through and do our part. He has provided the blueprints. Through our agency, we can create order for ourselves.

When our lives are in chaos, we feel out of sync with God's plan. We cannot think, plan well, or follow through. As President Ezra Taft Benson taught us, when we put first things first, "all other things fall into their proper place or drop out of our lives."[8] Yet sometimes we misinterpret the meaning of order. Mary Ellen Edmunds says: "First things first isn't only about importance. It's about order—what we do first, what we focus on and make time for and in which order. When I first read in the Doctrine and Covenants about creating 'a house of order, a house of God,' (D&C 88:119) I thought that meant that all the cupboards and closets and shelves in heaven were neat and orderly. Of course, it's more a matter of things happening at the right time and the right order, first things first."[9]

King Benjamin says it another way: "See that all these things are done in wisdom and order; for it is not requisite that a man [or woman] should run faster than he has strength . . . therefore, all things must be done in order" (Mosiah 4:27).

The order spoken of in the scriptures gives our lives eternal structure. As we prioritize and sort through what is really important, we will feel our Heavenly Father gently guiding our direction. When the routine of our lives is based on eternal structure, our house will be a house of order.

# A House of God

If we are to establish a house of God, we need to know who he is. In the words of President Gordon B. Hinckley, "God is the one sure source of truth. He is the fount of all inspiration. It is from him that the world must receive direction if peace is to come to the earth and if goodwill is to prevail among men. The earth is his creation. We are his children. Out of the love he bears for us, he will guide us if we seek, listen, and obey."[10]

Knowing God as "the one sure source of truth" directs us to have a house of God, especially in a world filled with increasing information we cannot trust. Our Heavenly Father has promised that his love will surround and protect us in our sincere efforts to prepare "every needful thing" as we establish our houses of prayer, faith, fasting, learning, glory, order, and, ultimately, a house of God.

In humility and gratitude I join with the Psalmist in saying:

> I will extol thee, O Lord; for thou hast lifted me up. . . .
> O Lord my God, I cried unto thee, and thou hast healed
> me. . . . Weeping may endure for a night, but joy cometh
> in the morning. . . . Thou hast turned for me my mourn-
> ing into dancing: thou hast put off my sackcloth, and
> girded me with gladness; To the end that my glory may
> sing praise to thee, and not be silent. O Lord my God, I
> will give thanks unto thee for ever." (Psalm 30:1, 2, 5, 11,
> 12)

# Notes

Janet Griffin Lee serves on the Young Women general board of The Church of Jesus Christ of Latter-day Saints. A graduate of Brigham Young University, she has taught elementary school but has spent most of the past thirty-four years as a full-time mother. She sits on the board of directors of Deseret Book Company and is the co-author of *Marathon of Faith*, which chronicles the nine years she and her late husband, Rex, spent dealing with his two cancers and other health challenges. The Lees are the parents of seven children and grandparents of seventeen.

1. Neal A. Maxwell, *One More Strain of Praise* (Salt Lake City: Bookcraft, 1999), p. 7.
2. Dallin H. Oaks, *Pure in Heart* (Salt Lake City: Bookcraft, 1988), p. 151.
3. Spencer W. Kimball, *The Miracle of Forgiveness* (Salt Lake City: Bookcraft, 1969), p. 98.
4. Jeffrey R. Holland, "'An High Priest of Good Things to Come,'" *Ensign*, November 1999, p. 36.
5. T. H. White, *The Once and Future King* (New York: G. P. Putnam's Sons, 1958), pp. 185–86.
6. *Teachings of Gordon B. Hinckley* (Salt Lake City: Deseret Book, 1997), p. 300.
7. C. S. Lewis, "The Weight of Glory," in *The Essential C. S. Lewis*, ed. Lyle W. Dorsett (New York: Touchstone, 1988), pp. 363, 368.
8. Ezra Taft Benson, "The Great Commandment—Love the Lord," *Ensign*, May 1988, p. 4.
9. Mary Ellen Edmunds, "It's about Time," in *Every Good Thing: Talks from the 1997 BYU Women's Conference* (Salt Lake City: Deseret Book, 1998), pp. 253–54.
10. Gordon B. Hinckley, *Be Thou an Example* (Salt Lake City: Deseret Book, 1981), p. 92.

# Chapter 4

# Lest Ye Forget

**KAREN SEDGWICK STONE**

*"Keep a history . . . of all things that transpire"* D&C 85:1

It was a beautiful Los Angeles June morning. My son Adam's UCLA graduation ceremony was under way when my sister-in-law handed me two pages from what appeared to be a diary. Glancing at it, I saw that my name was mentioned. I kept reading, and suddenly, I was eighteen again. I could almost hear the lapping of waves off Balboa Bay with a whiff of orange blossom mingling with the tang of salt and surf.

What I held in my hands was an excerpt from the life

history of Joe Barton, a friend from my youth. He was telling of a car accident—*a car accident that involved me!* He and his friend Bob West had breezed into my hometown of Riverside, California, that summer of 1952. I had just graduated from high school and was eagerly anticipating the new horizons that college would bring. Joe's account of a shared experience held me spellbound as he started out:

> When we went to church in Riverside that first Sunday, we met the stake president's daughters, Karen and Claudia Sedgwick. On church outings, Bob and I naturally spent time with these two girls. They both had beautiful singing voices *[I'm not enhancing this one bit!]*, and each of them played the ukulele. We'd sit around and sing for hours. *[Oh, do I remember! We sang everywhere with everybody.]*
>
> One Friday evening I had a date with Karen, and Bob had a date with a girl from the Newport Beach area. *[That was my best friend, Mary Joy, whom I had set up with Bob.]* We picked up Karen, drove over to Newport Beach for his date, then went to a movie and had a bite to eat. On the way back to Riverside, Karen continued talking to Bob, who was driving, while I drifted off. Apparently Bob drifted off too—because the next thing I knew, the car was tumbling! I could hear glass breaking and other frightful sounds around me. Dust was flying everywhere, and I was very scared.
>
> This was a serious accident, which absolutely destroyed Bob's car. The whole roof caved in [to] the top of the seats. . . . By the time someone actually forced the doors open, other motorists had stopped to help and gave us a ride into Riverside. The only person injured was Karen. She had a little scrape on her elbow that was bleeding slightly. . . . We were really lucky, except that Bob's car was totaled, and he had no insurance. It was a

late model Buick, and he lost the entire car as a result of that accident.[1]

The words ended as I replayed the dramatic sequence of events in my mind. Surely I couldn't have forgotten any of the vivid details of that accident! I do recall that the old Santa Ana Canyon Road was very dark. Back then it was orange groves all the way to the beach. And it *was* a miracle that no one was hurt as the car somersaulted, landing back on its wheels again—but my recollection was that we had continued to drive home in Bob's car after the accident—with only a few minor dents and maybe a broken side window! I would have recalled the car being totaled, motorists stopping and prying us out, and then being driven back to Riverside by someone else, wouldn't I? I don't even remember the scrape on my arm. Memory *is* selective—and what compelling reasons this suggests to document our lives as close to the event as possible!

Joe and Bob soon left town after that short summer of '52 (who could blame them?), but Mary Joy, or "M.J.," as she was known, who went on the double date that night, had been my friend since sixth grade. We shared many wonderful times, right up to her serving as one of my bridesmaids. A few years later found me deluged with diapers, dandelions, decorating, and drapes. Actually, my new home was devoid of drapes but strangely filled with goods galore for the Relief Society bazaar.

Despite all that, something compelled me to stop and put together one of the first true-life short stories I had ever composed up to that time. I found myself writing about the overwhelming gratitude I felt for M.J.'s example and the kind of friend she had been to me. Her sensitivity, as a nonmember, to my LDS values especially touched me. During spring break at the beach in about the eighth grade, I recounted, someone had started some cigarettes around a large circle of girls. *Everyone* was removing one and then passing the pack along . . . a pack that was inexorably making its way closer to me! My face flushed. I knew I could never take one—but how would everyone react when I refused? I didn't want to be conspicuous or to be thought a prude. Would they make fun of me? Would they still want to be my friends? None of that was even an issue when M.J. bravely handed the dreaded pack *past* me—nor did she take one. Because of her courageous show of support for me and my standards in the face of that often daunting peer pressure we all face as youth, it became much easier for me to stand out—and stand up—for what I believed.

My reminiscence was just three pages long, but would be the start of many such stories that have turned into my personal history—more than 250 pages worth! It became relatively easy, when I retired, to string together that tribute to Mary Joy with many other experiences that were bubbling up. They have told the story of my life so far, and this "short story" approach has worked best for me, though I've also kept daily journals and other assorted records through the years—though nothing like Wilford Woodruff's fifteen volumes over sixty-five years, or Spencer W. Kimball's eighty volumes of personal history. It was President Kimball who admonished: "We urge every person in the Church to keep a diary or a journal from youth up, all through his [or her] life."[2]

If you haven't been as diligent in this, don't despair; virtually any source can become part of a life history, from the annual Christmas letters that many families exchange to love letters. Other possibilities may consist of items found in a fam-

ily book of remembrance, journals (especially missionary journals), scrapbooks, Church talks, original poetry and songs,
obituaries, and, of course, diaries, memoirs, and life sketches
that may be in family hands. And don't forget the proverbial
treasure trove of memorabilia packed in the attic or boxed up
in the basement or garage. You can start with just about anything. What's important is to start! In whatever form, whether
long or short, prose or poetry, a personal history says: "I was
here. I am unique. I lived, loved, learned, laughed, suffered,
and conquered. My life mattered." And to paraphrase
Marshall McLuhan, perhaps the medium is also part of the
message.

This is certainly evident in the life of my father-in-law,
O. Leslie Stone, a no-nonsense, get-the-job-done kind of busi-
nessman and churchman—attributes that contributed in no
small part to his success. When "Father Stone" produced his
fifty-seven-page personal history, he did so, by dictation to his
secretary, in three days![3] That says as much about the man and
the way he accomplished things as anything.

Writing down your experiences can also be very revealing.
As shown, you can go back in time and relive experiences.
Writing can also clarify your thoughts. It's healthy and cathar-
tic to express the feelings and emotions you have lived
through. Mental health professionals use this unique power
of writing as a therapy tool to help clients "think straight" and
sort through challenging feelings and anxieties.

Everyone's life is a novel, it is said. We all have fascinating
stories to tell. Some may hesitate to write theirs down out of
modesty or shyness. They may think their lives have not been
particularly interesting, or could not be of interest to others.
Perhaps they think they couldn't "safely sell the family parrot

to the town gossip," as the old adage wryly warns. I don't mean to suggest that one must reveal *all* the "family secrets" or divulge events of an intensely personal nature. However, when one writes candidly, the record is inevitably more powerful.

English experts—professors and writers steeped in the most involved rhetoric and structure of our language—also concur that simplicity is preferred over complexity, even when complex concepts are conveyed. Consider the heartrending account of young Anne Frank as she and her family hid from the Nazis in World War II Amsterdam. Perhaps no other commentator among the many brilliant minds and writers of the Holocaust experience has achieved her command of emotion, sense of presence, and eloquence—and young Anne was barely a teenager and was simply writing in her diary!

Speaking to this topic, President Spencer W. Kimball said: "You are unique, and there may be incidents in your experience that are more noble and praiseworthy in their way than those recorded in any other life. There may be a flash of illumination here and a story of faithfulness there."[4]

The process of assembling our personal histories may include encouraging our parents, grandparents, and other family members and associates to tell about their "good old days." Their stories are our prologue. Interviews, videos, and tape recordings can all help ferret out fascinating information about loved ones—a process that by its very nature can link generations in new ways. Part of this has to do with the very essence of the gospel and the powerful spiritual forces that are unleashed when we participate in activities related to the threefold mission of the Church, in this case the redeeming of the dead (of which personal histories and journals are most decidedly a part). When my father retired and could more actively pursue his passion for genealogy, he was overjoyed when some of his grandchildren began sharing that same commitment. They had a bond with Grandpa like no others quite enjoyed when the spirit of Elijah took hold of them too. In this exciting pursuit that connects both sides of the veil, the influence of departed loved ones is renewed. They don't want to be forgotten any more than we do. Through our genealogical efforts we directly participate in the process of "turning the hearts of the fathers unto the children, and the hearts of the children unto the fathers, even those who are in heaven."[5] It's all part of a divinely ordained plan, one of the results of which is to help keep them "alive" to us.

Life histories of ancestors may also help uncover traits that have continued through the generations. My maternal grandmother, Amelia Jacobson Hansen, who was born in the United States in 1875 of Swedish parents shortly after they immigrated, could see a dress in a store window and duplicate it in no time—without a pattern. My granddaughter who is named for her, Dorothy Amelia, born 105 years later in 1980, has these very same interests and talents, and is currently studying textiles, weaving, and dressmaking in Sweden where her family resides.

Another interesting facet to life histories is rediscovering the lives of progenitors about whom we previously knew little, if anything. My grandmother on my father's side, Dora Belle Garrett Sedgwick, died when my father was just three years old, and almost nothing has been written of her. She died from complications of childbirth, and, sad to say, her infant died ten months later. In his personal history, my father wrote very little about his mother, though we know from her obituary that she was regarded as "one of Bountiful's noble and most respected citizens," for whose funeral businesses in Bountiful were closed, the service "fill[ing the Bountiful Tabernacle] to capacity . . . [in] one of the largest assemblies of the kind ever held [there]."[6] I know that Dad treasured a small picture of her. He said the only memory he had of his mother was at her death when grieving mourners surrounded her coffin. What a poignant first—and only—memory for a little boy to have of his mother!

When recently compiling some spiritually oriented stories from my family tree, I found that my great-aunt Lucy had recorded a most remarkable experience involving her sister Dora Belle. A faded copy of Lucy's life history, written by her daughters and aptly titled *Lest Ye Forget*, contains virtually the only reference we have unearthed so far about Grandmother Dora. Lucy's infant, Elizabeth, had died not long after Dora passed away. At the baby's funeral, grief-stricken Lucy fainted and could not be resuscitated. Her deathlike state was confirmed by a doctor who was present. She did not die, though later she said how much she had wanted to. However, during that experience Lucy apparently visited the spirit world in what appears to have been a near-death experience.

She revealed that she was able to see and talk to her sister Dora there, and described in detail how Dora arrived in a brilliant white carriage, and that she held two infants in her arms—one of them Lucy's. "I will take care of her, Lucy, until you come," Dora promised her sister. Lucy pleaded to remain, but was told it was not her time. She was revived and lived a long life, in which she often expressed the great comfort she derived from being permitted to see her infant in the care of her departed sister.

And what of the second child seen by Lucy in Dora's arms? Lucy observed that Dora was holding her own infant, Emily, who was still alive at that time. But not quite a year later, little Emily too passed away, joining her baby cousin Elizabeth in the arms of her loving mother, Dora—just as Lucy had been permitted to see.[7] What a void there would be in our already sparse family records about Grandma Dora if this beautiful and faith-promoting account hadn't been recorded. Lest *we* forget, indeed!

Though our progenitors' redemptive work is of primary importance and is the basis for our Latter-day Saint ancestral activity, the stories about them are what touch our hearts and remind us how much we miss them—or wish we had known them. The familial feelings and bonds that are generated from the reading and the writing of the inspirational and note-worthy aspects of their lives can make ancestors long gone as real to us as if they shared our lifetime. And how much sweeter the reunions we'll share when it is our time to depart this world and they are present to meet us in the next one!

One might well ask why, if "Angels above us are silent notes taking," as the hymn "Do What Is Right" declares, we really need to bother with this life history business. A careful reading of the lyrics, however, presents us with the sober facts: "Angels above us are silent notes taking *of ev'ry action.*"[8] This suggests they won't write our stories for us—they'll only record whether or not *we do!*

There is actually great personal satisfaction—delight, even—that can come from writing one's life story. A dear friend of mine feels she could never prepare hers because, as she explains, "I'm not a writer"—even though she is far from lacking interesting things to write about. Many charming, authentic, and fascinating histories have been written by "novices" and "amateurs." If a picture is worth a thousand words, then "Grandma" Moses (Anna Mary Moses, *nee* Robertson), the famous American primitive artist, who never had an art lesson, painted volumes. She didn't start painting until she was seventy-eight—when her fingers became too stiff to embroider! Even with that late start, she had a "career" that spanned twenty-three years, until her death in 1961 at the age of 101. Her country scenes remembered from her youth and life experiences possess a charm that landscapes by trained artists often lack, and her works today hang in museums the world over. It is interesting too that though she left behind a treasured legacy in her art, even she found the time to write her autobiography, published as *My Life's History* in 1952.[9]

It is sad that there are far too many Grandma Moseses who never picked up a paintbrush—or a pen. How many exemplary women's lives are now reduced to a line engraved on a tombstone, or a saying stitched onto a sampler or quilt, or maybe a few notes found in a recipe box? Imagine having only a birth, marriage, or death certificate to tell your life story! The epitaph on the grave of Judith Coffin in a Newbury, Massachusetts, cemetery dated 1705 hints at what must have been a full life:

> *Grave, sober, faithful, fruitfull vine was she,*
> *A rare example of true piety.*
> *Widow'd awhile she wayted wisht for rest*
> *With her dear husband in her Savior's breast.*[10]

Judith's headstone also states that she "lived to see 177 of her children and children's children to the 3d generation." No other written words remain to testify of the fine qualities that undoubtedly marked the eighty years of Judith Coffin. Those few lines have to speak for her eight decades.

Because of my mother's deep and abiding religious nature, if she had not sat *her* mother down to relate a spiritual manifestation she had as a young wife—*and then typed it up*—a wonderful, faith-promoting incident would be long forgotten. Soon after Amelia Jacobson Hansen was married and had given birth to her first child, her husband, Willard Hansen (my maternal grandfather), was called on a Church mission.[11] About that same time, Annie Christensen Hansen, Willard's stepmother, married to his father, Willard Snow Hansen, died. Annie left behind one-month-old Annie Elizabeth and four other small children—in addition to five older stepchildren, four of whom were still at home! (My grandfather Willard was the oldest of those five from his father's first wife, Maria.)[12]

Amelia was young, not quite twenty-two years of age, but didn't flinch from taking on the responsibility for that family. She moved to her father-in-law's large sheep ranch and dairy farm in Collinston, Utah, and nursed the one-month-old motherless infant, Annie Elizabeth, right along with her own two-month-old infant, Edna. "One cried all day and the other cried all night," Grandmother remembered. In addition, she cared for the other eight children and performed what must have been backbreaking work. That meant making everyone's clothing, "including shirts for Will's father and the boys," not to mention cleaning, washing, ironing, cooking all the meals, and performing all the other endless tasks associated with farm and ranch life. And this was at a time when

modern conveniences, let alone electricity, were rarely available. One can hardly imagine her feelings the first night there,
without her husband, in isolated country, with the numbing
reality setting in. Amelia related:

> I dozed off to sleep and distinctly saw Annie, who
> had just died. Whether in a dream or vision, I don't
> know, but I saw her standing off the floor. She smiled at
> me with a very pleased expression on her face which I felt
> was [due to my] taking care of her infant. I have always
> remembered that smile. . . . Later that same night I was
> awakened by a mountain lion that moaned and screamed
> like a dying woman, directly under my window. I
> couldn't move a muscle. I was alone with two tiny babies
> in the room where Annie had died. When morning fi-
> nally came, I expected to see my hair had turned white.[13]

Grandmother Amelia had earlier dictated a very brief life
history, but it consisted of just basic facts—none of the heart
and soul of her life. How grateful I am to have this additional
insight into her experience!

In their seventies, my mother and dad wrote their personal histories. They're equally fascinating to read because
they each include as much *life* as *history!* From the many experiences Mother details, a pattern emerges that clearly speaks
of her priorities and values. "We're told that the angels envy
men their ability both to forgive and to repent," Hugh Nibley
has commented.[14] Mother took this concept to heart when she
taught us, "When you learn how to forgive you really learn
how to love!" By that she meant, of course, the love that is the
pure love of Christ, even charity, as referred to in Moroni
7:45–48. Mother learned this early in her marriage—and liber-
ally passed the lesson on to us (repetition was definitely not

one of her weaknesses) via an incident that has come to be known in our family lore as "The Apple Pie Story."

My mother and father, Lola Mae Hansen and Joel Garrett Sedgwick, were very different people. In their later years, those differences tamed considerably and became a delightful part of their relationship that we all cherished. Just how different they were, however, must have made for an interesting adjustment period in the early stage of their marriage when the "irresistible force" of Mother hit the "immovable object" of Dad. Such was the case, as Mother relates in her history, when they had their first quarrel:

> I was six months pregnant, felt miserable, and still couldn't keep food on my stomach. Joel came home from a hard day working to a very upset house. All of our belongings were piled in the middle of the floor. I was Oh so tired and longed for nothing more than a long rest. He went to take a shower, came back into the room and said, "Where is my clean underwear?" In the process of moving I had neglected to do our laundry. After learning this fact, he said in a voice which rubbed me the wrong way and made my Swedish wrath rise, "Huh! I should think a wife could at least have clean underwear for her husband when he needs it!"
>
> That did it. I mustered all the dignity I could command in my delicate condition, looked him straight in the eye, and said, "I didn't marry you to be your valet." I walked out of the room and slammed the door. I spent a miserable night on the living room couch. In the morning, a wall of silence separated us, as high as a mountain. Believe me, I wasn't going to be the first to break it down. [Joel] left without breakfast, and if I'd had enough money I would have gone back to Mother in Salt Lake City.

There was only one problem with this solution—it was not

available to her. Her very own mother wouldn't have let her in the door! The "Beat or Cheat" rule was well known among Grandma Amelia's four daughters: "Unless your husbands beat you or leave you for other women, you are not welcome back home. When you marry that man, you make a go of it!" Mother, being Mother, also considered the eternal ramifications:

> I began thinking of the vows I had made in the temple. I married this man for time and all eternity. I couldn't go through *eternity* without speaking to him! I decided the least I could do was wash his underwear, which I did. Then, as I cleaned our new little home and brought order out of confusion, I remembered how he liked the apple pie my mother had taught me to bake, and I decided to make him one for dinner. As I peeled the apples and made the pie dough, I discovered a great truth—that if you do something nice for the person you are angry with, the anger completely leaves you, and you realize and understand how much you have been at fault.
>
> Joel came home to an orderly home, clean underwear, and a well-cooked dinner. But the mountain of silence was still there until I brought on the apple pie. He then broke it by saying, "You do still love me, don't you?" And he gave me a big kiss. Oh the joy of making up, and being happy again! To this day, when I make an apple pie, Joel wonders what he has done. . . . That mountain of silence is deadly to a happy marriage. I have tried since to be the first to break it down.[15]

My parents have now passed away and their voices are stilled, but their words are vibrantly alive through their histories. Mother was especially known for bearing a fervent, glowing, and even dramatic testimony—whenever and wherever she could—of the truth of the gospel of Jesus Christ. It was with this unshakable witness that she concluded her history, making her testimony available "to my beloved children, my grandchildren and my great grandchildren and my great great great grandchildren." That is so like Mother—but she meant every word of it, just as she did her testimony:

"I have a deep testimony and conviction in my heart, and know as I live and breathe, that Jesus is the Christ, and my elder brother. I believe that some day I shall see my Savior if I can endure to the end and keep all of his commandments to the best of my ability, which I shall try to do. . . . May we all be united in the name and love of our Savior, Jesus Christ."[16] In true testimony meeting fashion, she even added the "Amen."

A little later, Mother included an addendum to her history, which, of course, called for another conclusion with yet another testimony. This one, however, truly would be her last, as far as her written word is concerned:

"As I finish this addition to my Life Story, again, I leave to my children and their families my deepest love and affection. I want them all to seek and find the greatest joy and happiness in the world which can only come by living their temple covenants, and, to 'walk in the path of the low valley and be strict in the plain road.'

*"I believe that love is the strongest force in the world. To understand and live its many facets is life's greatest adventure."*[17]

I don't know that Mother fully recognized that those would be her "final words," written as they were on a back page already crowded with family photos and put together almost as an afterthought, with just enough space for her second testimony. Knowing Mother, I suspect she had several more addenda and testimonies planned! And yet I can't think of a better "last will and testimony" for her to have left than the one she did: a literal testimony of the love that so permeated her being.

President Kimball, remarking on how vital record keeping is in the gospel plan, said, "I want to tell you it is very important, so important that when the Lord, himself, came to the Nephites as recorded in 3 Nephi, he said to Nephi, who was the chief of the twelve disciples there, 'Let me see your records.'"[18]

At their best, inspirational personal histories can be thought of as a type of personal scripture. Perhaps, then, the canon of scripture is the family history for us all. When Nephi begins his account, "having been born of goodly parents" and "make[s] a record of [his] proceedings in [his] days" (1 Nephi 1:1), he is creating an account both of himself and of his family on their amazing journey to the Promised Land. The fact that his was also a lineage that was destined to populate the New World and be led by the Lord through prophets and apostles as a branch of the tribe of Joseph, with the ultimate visitation by Christ, elevates it to scripture, even "Another Testament of Jesus Christ." How fortunate we are to have that record from a time when record keeping was not an easy process.

Indeed, the Lord places such a high value on records, and their place as the very foundation of righteous society, that he sanctioned the removal of Laban as being a better alternative "that one man should perish than that a nation should dwindle and perish in unbelief" (1 Nephi 4:13). The Book of Mormon itself presents a case history of this very phenomenon with the Mulekites, who came to the New World not long after Lehi and founded the land and mighty city of Zarahemla. In what is certainly an object lesson on the importance of the written word, because they brought no records their language and religion became corrupted—even to the degree of their forming an atheistic society. Only upon Mosiah's instructing them in their once-shared language could the two peoples even communicate (see Omni 1:12–19). The Mulekite history was then recorded, and how fascinating it would be to study their chronicles. Perhaps someday we will.

The complete record of the Jaredites, abridged as the book of Ether, presents similar food for thought. Moroni declared he was unable to write "the hundredth part" of their voluminous history (Ether 15:33). What an incredible addition to the body of scripture if we had the other "99 percent" of the Jaredite records! It is interesting that Nephi's account itself was not intended to be the beginning of the Book of Mormon—his father Lehi's was. Given the rich scriptural, historical, and cultural treasures that comprise the fifteen books of Mormon—*plates of gold* in the truest sense—we can only imagine what "pearls of great price" would have been found in the book of Lehi. As it is, perhaps two-thirds of the Book of Mormon was sealed and is yet to come forth. But we are thankful we have what we have—and how diligently do we search those scriptures?

The four gospels of the New Testament provide a biblical analog to this. The complementary, interwoven nature of the gospels is referred to by theologians as the *harmony of the gospels*. The term has specific reference to how well each gospel account confirms and supports the narrative of the others as they essentially tell the same story. Equally fascinating is what each gospel *uniquely* contributes to the "greatest story ever told." An examination of the New Testament outline reveals that if it were not for Luke, we would have no other record of the miraculous and prophetic birth of John the Baptist to Mary's cousin Elisabeth (Luke 1:5–25), nor know of the Annunciation of Mary (Luke 1:26–56). If not for Matthew, Joseph's visitation by the angel declaring Mary's child to be the Son of God would be entirely missing, nor would we have the visit of the Magi, nor the flight into Egypt (Matthew 2:1–12, 13–18). John provides our only witness to the marriage in Cana, where water was turned into wine (John 2:1–11), and his is the sole account of the woman at the well to whom Christ taught the lesson of drawing from spiritual waters from which no one ever thirsts (John 4:5–45). Mark gives us our only telling of the parable of the seed growing secretly (Mark 4:26–29). Without Luke we would have no parable of the Good Samaritan (10:25–37), the Prodigal Son (15:11–32), or the Lord's Prayer (11:1–13).[19] And on it goes.

Perhaps we'll never know how important this all is until we move to our third estate and can there perceive in spiritual dimensions we're simply not capable of here. Maybe there we will recognize the importance of the written word, its relationship to the sealing power of Elijah, and its ultimate connection to Deity itself. Ponder the words of Hugh Nibley on the phenomenon of the written word:

> Writing itself is the most—as Galileo says . . . the most marvelous device ever invented. He says, "No invention will ever approach writing for sophistication and the marvelous things it does. To transfer knowledge and telling and emotion over thousands of years through any distance in space." It beats TV or anything else you could possibly devise. It's marvelous! "And [to] do that," he says, "with 24, 26 little symbols, very simple designs. . . ." That's given by the finger of the Lord, you see.[20]

We have a shining glimpse of this in John chapter one,

verse one, where the power of the language virtually transcends itself in scriptural form to combine with the power of the concept itself:

> *In the beginning was the Word,*
> *and the Word was with God,*
> *and the Word was God.*

We all have life stories worth telling—and we are commanded to tell those stories. As the literal children of God, perhaps we'll someday recognize not only that our histories are priceless and a tribute to him who made us but also that our very writing of them is part of the process by which we are written into the Lamb's Book of Life. And in this way we can obtain the blessings of that which the Book itself represents and promises, even the work and the glory of God:

> *to bring to pass*
> *the immortality and eternal life*
> *of man.*
> *(Moses 1:39)*

## Notes

Karen Sedgwick Stone was born and raised in Riverside, California, of goodly parents, Lola Hansen and Joel Garrett Sedgwick. Married to the late Douglas Leslie Stone, she was widowed with three children at the age of twenty-eight. An educator by profession, Karen has been both a BYU faculty member in home economics education and a specialist with the Utah State Office of Education. Teaching assignments in the Church have been among Karen's favorite callings, from early-morning seminary to Gospel Doctrine. Karen has served as a stake or ward Relief Society president four times, and may continue to do so until she "gets it right."

1. Joseph Barton, "Life After College," in *Personal History*. Unpublished; used by permission.

2. Spencer W. Kimball, October 1977 general conference, as cited in "Journals," *Encyclopedia of Mormonism*, 4 vols., ed. Daniel H. Ludlow (New York: MacMillan, 1992), pp. 770–71. The entire article is an excellent one for the background it provides on the essential LDS practice of journal writing. See also "Record Keeping."

3. O. Leslie Stone, *O. Leslie Stone History: Covering Years 1903–1960*, June 1960. Unpublished typescript in author's possession.

4. *The Teachings of Spencer W. Kimball*, ed. Edward L. Kimball (Salt Lake City: Bookcraft, 1982), p. 351.

5. Bruce R. McConkie, "Elijah the Prophet," in *Mormon Doctrine* (Salt Lake City: Bookcraft, 1958), p. 207.

6. Joel Garrett Sedgwick, *History of, Events in and Recollections from The Life of Joel Garrett Sedgwick, by Himself* (1979), p. 2. Unpublished typescript in author's possession. (The obituary, reprinted in Dad's history, is from the *Deseret News*, 13 February 1907.)

7. Ruth Barlow Green, Velma Barlow, *"Lest Ye Forget," Life History of Lucy Ann Garrett Barlow (5/7/1881–10/31/1962)*. Unpublished typescript in author's possession.

8. *Hymns*, no. 237; emphasis added.

9. Edwin L. Fulwider, "Moses, 'Grandma,'" *World Book Encyclopedia* (Chicago: Field Enterprises Educ. Corp., 1968), p. 683.

10. Laurel Thatcher Ulrich, *Good Wives, Images and Reality in the Lives of Women in Northern New England, 1650–1750* (New York: Vintage Books, June 1991), pp. 146–52. This fascinating account nonetheless extrapolates a wealth of information about Judith Coffin and the lives of many others from colonial New England *precisely because* of family stories and anecdotes that have been handed down and eventually recorded.

11. Even though this was in the 1890s, a generation past the pioneer era, it was not uncommon for married men with young families to be called on Church missions—a feat made even more remarkable because of the challenging conditions under which they often left their families.

12. The relationships can get a little confusing in this family because of the four separate wives of Willard Snow Hansen, each of whom had different sets of children, numbering twenty altogether!

13. Amelia Jacobson Hansen, Personal History addendum. Unpublished typescript in author's possession.

14. Hugh Nibley, footnoted and annotated transcript of *The Faith of an Observer: Conversations with Hugh Nibley*, film documentary (Provo, Utah: F.A.R.M.S., 1985), p. 15.

15. Lola Sedgwick, *The Life Story of Lola Mae Hansen Sedgwick* (1980–81), p. 9. Unpublished typescript in author's possession. An account of Mother's "Apple

Pie Story" was published in Helen Ream Bateman's delightful book, *Roots & Wings* (Salt Lake City: Deseret Book, 1983), pp. 5–7. Mother also had two stories published in Marjie Calhoun Jensen's *When Faith Writes the Story* (Salt Lake City: Bookcraft, 1973). One concerned a dramatic spiritual experience that she underwent; the other related an incident of divine intervention that occurred to her father and grandfather that involved the uncovering of hundreds of genealogical records from their native Denmark.

16. Lola Sedgwick, *Life Story*, p. 18.

17. Ibid., p. 31; emphasis added. The quotation she makes about the "low valley" and "plain road" is from 2 Nephi 4:32, part of what is sometimes referred to as the "Psalm of Nephi." It was one of Mother's favorites—and oh, how she could quote it!

18. *Teachings of Spencer W. Kimball*, p. 476. President Kimball's reference is to 3 Nephi 23:7 and is found there as "Bring forth the record which ye have kept."

19. See David H. Yarn, Jr., *The Four Gospels As One* (New York: Harper, 1961), pp. 189–201.

20. Nibley, *Faith of an Observer*, p. 11. Nibley expounds extensively to this fascinating concept of the "Promethean" aspects of writing in his essay "The Genesis of the Written Word." Used with permission.

# Chapter 5

# Wounds of the Heart

**SALLY H. BARLOW**

*"That [ye] shall be healed" D&C 124:104*

Lauren hated life. She felt left behind by her husband, who had now retired but seemed even busier with hobbies than he had been with his career. She felt discarded by her children, since they had started lives of their own. She found herself increasingly tired, put upon by neighbors, family, Church jobs. Every day brought more depression; she "despaired even of life" (2 Corinthians 1:8); and she was discovering more aches and pains as her body seemed to turn on

her with arthritis, headaches, stomachaches, and sleep distur-
bances.

Her doctors tried to help control her symptoms, but after
several years of going from one doctor to another she felt like
an "old woman" with only vague complaints that apparently
couldn't be cured even by reputable doctors. The last M.D.
she had visited suggested that a consultation with a psychia-
trist might be helpful. She countered that her symptoms were
not in her head! The doctor tried to explain that the mind and
the body were in concert, and that sometimes uncovering
psychological pain helped alleviate physical symptoms. Her
health-care plan had recently updated its availability of mental health coverage. Still, she couldn't bring herself to go to a
therapist. Only crazy people did that.

Her symptoms worsened, and she spent more and more
time in bed. She realized one day, while struggling to figure
out what was at the root of her problems, that she didn't
know how to be responsible for her own happiness. She had
never really known.


Lei had worked hard all her life. She had been widowed
early and had never remarried. She had prided herself on her
ability to work long hours efficiently, care for her aging mother
who lived with her, and keep up all her Church callings. Even
her garden was the envy of the neighborhood. But recently
she was plagued with vague uneasiness. She couldn't believe
it was merely a result of changes in her hormones now that
she had entered that strange time of "perimenopause."

She had been dating a man in the area who was pressing
her to consider marriage. She really liked him but just
couldn't bring herself to say yes. Her mother's health prob-

lems and her grown children's struggles seemed to weigh upon her more and more heavily. She felt as if she had "a thorn in the flesh" (2 Corinthians 12:7) to humble her, but unlike Paul, she couldn't understand what was truly wrong and why she was suffering so. She asked for a blessing from her bishop. She was surprised when he felt impressed to tell her to forgive her grandfather.

Lucy had never married. She prided herself on being able to do just about anything she had set her mind to. Having been a professional woman all her adult life, she made a comfortable income, had invested her money wisely, and was looking forward to retirement. But when her office partner asked her if she might want to retire early to take full advantage of her remaining years, she realized she was unsure what to do. At the same time, her stake president asked her to be the stake Relief Society president.

The sisters in the stake's seven wards had diverse circumstances and included those who had recently emigrated from economically struggling countries. She prayed fervently for direction—being torn between taking her retirement money and traveling, and organizing the sisters to truly help each other. Instead of the clear answer she had hoped for, Lucy became quietly aware that she held a deep-seated fear of people from different races, economic circumstances, and cultures.

These women all have in common their dissatisfaction with later life. From the descriptions it may be difficult to tell which woman is rich or poor, white or of color, tall or short, or any other particularity. These aspects of diversity might be influential in their circumstances in a number of ways, and may serve as the mold that sets the shape of their particular distress, but the basic ingredients of dissatisfaction with change of life-cycle circumstances that go into that mold are the same. Women's later life-cycle issues specifically entail such things as retirement, financial security, widowhood, and well-being which are often influenced by how we feel about these transitions—are they gradual, abrupt, imposed, chosen?[1]

The most important thing that these women all have in common is that they are members of The Church of Jesus Christ of Latter-day Saints, which invites women into a sisterhood that is unparalleled in its power and organization anywhere else in the world or in any other time on earth. They know that God's eternal plan includes two distinct facets: moving through seasons of life in order to gain experience; and the attainment of joy. Their particular distresses, however, are interfering with their ability to weather these seasons and find joy and happiness.

Many people bear unseen burdens, or perhaps unhealed wounds within their souls. The Lord teaches us that the soul is the spirit *and* the body (see D&C 88:15). Unreconciled wounds may actually damage both our spirit and our body because wounds carry the power to interfere with our mental and physical growth, and therefore our mortal and immortal identity. There is clear evidence from medical science that the mind and the body are in a mutual influence cycle, and we know from modern revelation that our earthly existence is inextricably linked to our premortal selves, and both will be influential as we enter the next estate after the death of the body.

Before coming to the peace necessary for a secure

foundation in Christ, we may need to reexamine these wounds. Through prayer, priesthood power, and perhaps professional help, we can look forward to the true healing found in Christ. Elder Neal A. Maxwell reminds us that Christ will help us through our afflictions:

> When we take Jesus' yoke upon us, this admits us eventually to what Paul called the "fellowship of [Christ's] sufferings" (Philippians 3:10). Whether illness or aloneness, injustice or rejection, . . . our comparatively small-scale sufferings, if we are meek, will sink into the very marrow of the soul. We then better appreciate not only Jesus' sufferings for us, but also His matchless character, moving us to greater adoration and even emulation. Alma revealed that Jesus knows how to succor us in the midst of our griefs and sicknesses (see Alma 7:11–12). He knows them firsthand; thus His empathy is earned.[2]

## *Wounds*

What is a "wound"? According to the dictionary, a wound is "an injury . . . due to external violence . . . rather than disease; an injury or hurt to feelings, sensibilities, reputation."[3] We know there are physical wounds that we can usually see, and there are psychological, emotional, or mental wounds that we generally cannot see. These are not visible to the human eye. But there are many ways in which the human psyche keeps unreconciled hurts "alive" in us that are actually visible by way of demonstrable symptoms: depression, sleep disorders, psychosomatic distress (chronic headaches, backaches, and other body aches that do not seem to go away even with proper medical attention and are not the result of physical illnesses). These wounds can come from a variety of sources. Sometimes things can go wrong—from accidents to the exercise of the agency of others that may harm us (neglect or abuse from childhood, spouse abuse, divorce) to problems stemming from our own misuse of agency (eating disorders, chemical dependency).

## Aging

Some people experience aging itself as a wound! Much of the psychological literature that examines issues of aging—variously titled by such words as "gerontological studies, eldering, the greying of America"—suggest an array of concerns during this stage, including increased depression, sleep disorders, memory problems. There are contradictions that exist in this empirical literature (for instance, there is an ongoing argument whether depression leads to sleep disorders or the reverse, whether memory problems are real, and so on). It is important to point out that the most current theories on aging are no longer dominated by a "deficiency model," which used to state that aging was inevitably full of physical and mental decline. Aging is now considered part of the life cycle, and the current theories are taking their lead from the seminal work of Erik Erikson, who has suggested that each stage of life presents its own challenges and crises to be overcome, and when combined with the most current theories suggests a course that moves through mourning from losses, giving meaning to past and present experiences, accepting one's past and present states, (re)establishing self-coherence and self-continuity, and achieving ego integration.[4]

Recently, the ninth biennial congress of the International Psychogeriatric Association concluded that the quality of life for an aging population was an imperative "just as vexing and worthy as longevity itself. . . . We are living longer, but are we living better?"[5]

The aging process appears to be that part of mortal experience that presents us with a number of paradoxes illustrated by the following well-known statements: "Youth is wasted on the young," "Too soon old, too late smart." It appears that when we are wise enough to put our knowledge to good use, our bodies are too tired; when we have finally figured out how to be good parents, our children have grown; when we have finally mastered a number of intellectual domains, no one listens to us anymore because the next generation commands attention in the workplace. Yet these dilemmas illustrate the limits of the world's knowledge. Perhaps these seeming paradoxes are just God's plan to take advantage of every angle that will enhance our growth. As members of The Church of Jesus Christ of Latter-day Saints we know that mortal experience is a school, a time in which we "must grow in grace and in the knowledge of the truth" (D&C 50:40).

As we become "earthly older" we pass through predictable stages. Often we are so busy just surviving children, work, and other demanding issues during those years that we do not have time to consider the wounds we might have suffered in early life. But during our later years we may have time to reflect. And even if we do not have time to reflect, given many of the recent changes in the status of older adults who are often actively involved in childcare, elder care, and employment, it still might be worth contemplation. There are interesting parallels between trauma and aging, since the developmental tasks of aging are the very same tasks required of people recovering from trauma: dealing with loss, constructing meaning out of the event that allows us to make sense of it so we can go on, accepting what happened, establishing a sense of self-consistency and coherence, and achieving a sense of self-integration.[6]

## Aging and Trauma

Classic examples of the price exacted by early wounds can be found in the diagnosis Posttraumatic Stress Disorder (PTSD, see Table 1). PTSD has been studied especially in relation to men and women returning from war. Although a disproportionate amount of research was conducted on the Vietnam War PTSD veterans, it has been found recently that many World War II veterans as well as women who have been traumatized by events other than war suffer from PTSD as well. Because less emphasis was placed on these groups, many of them have often suffered in silence.

Rape, incest, assault, war—many other traumas work their way inside of us so that we do not know how to let love in later. This becomes problematic for a number of reasons. There is empirical data suggesting that when these wounds come from the very people we expect to care for us, we may be even more harmed than if the wound comes from a stranger.[7] There is also evidence to suggest that being subjected to random violence (terrorism, drunk drivers) also takes its toll.[8] Thus, PTSD can result from such unreconciled traumas, whether from random or predictable acts of strangers or intimates. Also, though a person may not meet all the criteria for PTSD, any diminution of the quality of life caused by unresolved wounds that could be ameliorated should be attempted. We must remember that the subjective experience of wounds is just that, subjective. An unkind word spoken long ago by a loved one may have wounded us so deeply that it acts the same as a terrorist bomb.

"If I haven't dealt with it so far, why bother now?" The data regarding individual responses to trauma is variable, but there is some evidence that a delayed onset or exacerbation of PTSD may actually occur during the process of aging.[9] Over time if we have not adequately dealt with a trauma, we begin to experience decreased abilities to cope and an increased focus on negative life events. Often, we can put off such reckoning by concentrating on occupational concerns, childcare, and so on. However, "In the effort to adapt to aging, traumatic experiences that have not been worked through may surface."[10] Bad memories simply do not disappear. For whatever reason, God has organized our brains in such a fashion that these events are stored, not deleted.

Sometimes facing these traumas is especially difficult because the trouble happened when we were young. It can also be difficult because we may be in contact with the person with whom we feel unreconciled, as in cases of incest or spouse abuse that have not resulted in familial alienation or divorce, respectively. Sincere pleading with the Lord will yield direction. Priesthood blessings will help. Some women avoid this level of help because their trauma happened at the hands of an unworthy priesthood holder, and they have generalized their fear to all males. Nevertheless, it is helpful to pour our hearts out to Heavenly Father and to avail ourselves of all the priesthood blessings regardless of the pains inflicted by a few. The Lord sees us as we truly are, in times of triumph or despair. His sincerest wish is to light our path if we will just ask, "For behold, this is my work and my glory—to bring to pass the immortality and eternal life of man" (Moses 1:39). Joseph Smith wrote, "Happiness is the object and design of our existence; and will be the end thereof, if we pursue the path that leads to it, and this path is virtue, uprightness, faithfulness, holiness, and keeping all the commandments of God."[11]

## The Process of Reconciliation

War, trauma, rape, despair, unhappiness—how do we cope? There is a huge body of research on the many and varied ways to recover from depression, despair, or trauma. The one thing many researchers agree on is that a person's *attitude* about such events, or about one's stage of life, often determines his or her subsequent quality of life. Dysfunctional attitudes (one's general outlook) may make a person vulnerable to depression, to dissatisfaction. In addition, a person's attributional style (one's causal explanation) may also contribute, due to various beliefs about what causes ill health, or sadness.[12] For instance, when people really believe they have no control over their own lives and behave accordingly (letting others make their decisions, expecting the worst, and so forth), it isn't surprising that they are unhappy. There is a robust self-help literature backed up by research literature that spells out step by step how to overcome such thinking styles.[13] There are also numerous inspiring accounts in popular literature about people who have recovered from terrible events. Reconciliation is possible.

Paul and Timothy counseled the people of Corinth, "Be ye reconciled to God" (2 Corinthians 5:20). Our prophet Gordon B. Hinckley has stated, "There is no peace in the reflecting on the pain of old wounds. There is peace only in repentance and forgiveness. This is the sweet peace of the Christ, who said, 'blessed are the peacemakers: for they shall be called the children of God' (Matt. 5:9)."[14] Reconciliation of past wounds may require many strategies—priesthood blessings, prayer, family help. When we are in the very center of the pain, however, it is difficult to feel God's love; it is difficult to hearken to the counsel of our leaders. This attitude may constitute a form of pouting—a sense that our pain is worse than anyone else's, that people just don't understand. As harsh as this may sound, Elder Neal A. Maxwell reminds us that "pouting, even sophisticated pouting will not change reality. It does no good either, to withhold oneself from the fray wishing things were otherwise."[15]

Part of the work as we travel this path toward reconciliation may involve forgiveness. This does not mean that we pretend bad things haven't happened. Nor does it mean that we can't pass judgment on these events. Elder Dallin H. Oaks reminds us that we are *required* to make what he labels "intermediate judgments" during our lives (for example, "What happened to me was a terrible thing inflicted upon me by a person acting sinfully or illegally"). He contrasts this with what he calls "final judgments" ("That person will go to hell"). We must turn this advice upon ourselves as well and avoid making final judgments toward ourselves ("I will never be able to overcome the trauma that has happened to me. I have failed"). But by the same token, we will need to make intermediate judgments ("A bad thing has happened to me. I seem unable to break through this on my own. Perhaps I should seek professional help"). Elder Oaks reminds us that "we should seek the guidance of the Spirit in our decisions. We should limit our judgment to our own stewardship . . . [and base our judgments upon] adequate knowledge of the facts. . . . As far as possible, we should judge circumstances rather than people . . . [and] apply righteous standards."[16] Finally, we must remember the commandment given to us, "I, the Lord will forgive whom I will forgive, but of you it is required to forgive all men" (D&C 64:10).

This may seem like a tall order when forgiveness is the last thing on our minds—especially when anger may have been stage-appropriate or helpful for a time, as in the case of the traumatized victim whose anger helps her exit a life-threatening experience. But anger is hard to hang onto for-ever. The Lord only asks us to do those things that will bene-fit us in the long run. Surely there is something wise about finding a way to rid ourselves of the canker of hatred, even if it is justified. Additionally, there has been a resurgence in the empirical literature that examines the salutary effects of reli-gion generally, and tried-and-true religious tenets specifically, such as forgiveness. In a recent psychological study compar-ing incest victims who utilized "forgiveness therapy" with those who utilized more "traditional" therapy, the clients who followed the carefully devised steps toward forgiveness recovered more quickly.[17] Though it may not feel possible at first as we begin the journey of reconciliation, we may have blessings poured out upon us as we rid our souls of weighty anger, cankering ugly memories, and depressing phobias that may have developed in response to the early traumas. In fact, Elder Neal A. Maxwell reminds us of the unimaginable bless-ings that are in store for us if we but "surrender to God. At that moment the universe becomes a vast home, rather than a majestic but hostile maze. Surprisingly with such surrender comes victory. . . . To yield to him is to receive *all* that he has!"[18]

Soliciting the help of a skilled professional may be an appropriate step if, regardless of the efforts made on our behalf from priesthood leaders, we still feel stuck. It is always important to select a therapist who will not mishandle our belief system[19] or put "false" memories in our minds. This is currently a huge controversy in the psychological literature that can be summarized quickly here as the battle between those who believe false memories really can be put into suggestible clients by unskilled therapists versus those who believe that people really can uncover trauma from their past and that such memories are an accurate reflection of past events. Most professionals are aware of this controversy, and if they have been expertly trained they know how to be helpful to those who have suffered distressing events. (See Table 2 as a guideline about how to select a therapist.) Surely doing something difficult in the short run to aid our recovery in the long run will be worth it. Ignoring the problem, knowing it is there but staying stuck because we feel sorry for ourselves or unable to help ourselves will not help us be all that we are meant to be. We may even feel very justified in this stance— after all, who could blame us for feeling this way when such unfair things have happened to us. If our goal were justification, this kind of attitude would be acceptable. But sanctification, not merely justification, is our true goal.

## Christ-Centered Solutions

At the beginning of this chapter we were introduced to the stories of three women united by their common bond of despair. Fortunately, Lauren, Lei, and Lucy found the courage to change. Lauren decided to get help. Against all the prejudices she had held about "those people who went to shrinks," she decided to make an appointment with the psychotherapist and see if she could get to the root of the problem. She was determined not to waste the years of mortality she had left. She discovered through long and painful discussions that she really had never learned how to rely upon her own resources. She had been raised to let others make decisions, and though this style worked for a long time it was no longer working now that she needed to decide how to enrich her life. Her newfound independence caused a few temporary wrinkles in her relationship with her husband, who was surprised at the changes she had undergone. As they struggled together, however, their marriage became strengthened through honest communication, a more fulfilling sex life, and genuine fun. He began to seek out her company, and she realized how much she loved him and why she had married him! She began to experience fewer and fewer annoying physical symptoms as she learned to speak up when she was upset (instead of letting her symptoms "speak" for her with loud headaches and so on). She also found a way to treat her body more respectfully by engaging in physical activity and eating healthy food. Now that she was an active participant, life held more joy than it had ever held before when she had been but a passive bystander.

Lei entered a time of great reflection. She paid attention to her thoughts, her dreams, and her fears instead of constantly being distracted by the business of a thousand tasks. She read her journals from when she was a child, and finally let herself remember the painful memories of a time in her life when her grandfather had sexually abused her. At the time she had felt as though she could tell no one, and when she got older she decided just not to think about it. But between childhood and later adulthood a lot had happened. Her fear of men, her reluctance to get close to anyone after her husband died, had roots in her troubled relationship with her grandfather. Though she greatly enjoyed her children and grandchildren, she realized she was often overwhelmed with fears that they too might be subjected to molestation, thus she was hyper-vigilant about anything that might go wrong, which destroyed the quality of their interactions. Her relationship with her mother had also been strained all these years, and she contemplated whether or not her mother had been abused by her own father, Lei's grandfather. She had invited the Spirit of the Holy Ghost to attend her always, and on one particular day she realized she was being impressed to speak to her mother about the abuse. Together they shared many painful memories of encounters with this man who had apparently hurt them both. Reconciled to each other, and to their lives, they began to get along better. When Lei's mother quietly passed away in her sleep several months later, Lei felt at peace and she began to make new plans.

Lucy decided to spend thoughtful reflection on her deep-seated prejudices. She talked to her siblings and examined ways in which she had learned certain attitudes toward people of different races. She prayed to her Father in Heaven to help her uncover the seeds of hatred and fear. He answered her. Eventually she did decide to retire. She had given all she really wanted to give to the "world of work." However, instead of traveling right away, she told her bishop she would love to help the stake work creatively to solve the many needs

SALLY H. BARLOW

of the sisters in her area. As stake Relief Society president she began to organize service groups whose sole purpose was to aid struggling people in other countries. Some of the sisters were able to help people from their own homelands. In the midst of a very successful campaign to bring much-needed medicine to a small African country torn by civil strife, she was invited by the village elders to bring the supplies in person. Lucy had never been so grateful for sufficient income that allowed her to go. She realized with great joy that she was traveling *and* serving, a combination she had never thought possible. And she was traveling to a country whose people had once frightened her. Her brothers and sisters no longer seemed to be certain colors—they were all one in the light of Christ.

## Summary

"We are troubled on every side, yet not distressed; we are perplexed, but not in despair; persecuted, but not forsaken; cast down, but not destroyed" (2 Corinthians 4:8–9). As humans, we are involved in a great work that includes the challenges of mortality and the promise of eternity. In this second estate we undergo the developmental processes known as aging that often present us with overwhelming demands requiring creative problem solving and increased reliance on the Lord. As Joseph Smith was told, "Thine adversity and thine afflictions shall be but a small moment" (D&C 121:7). And as God had Isaiah tell Israel, "For a small moment have I forsaken thee, but with great mercies will I gather thee" (Isaiah 54:7). In order to overcome some of the more troubling challenges, those unresolved wounds inflicted by others or by ourselves upon ourselves, we must struggle to see time through God's perspective: "For our light affliction, which is but for a moment, worketh for us a far more exceeding and eternal weight of glory" (2 Corinthians 4:17). This weight of glory may be more easily borne on shoulders broadened by adversity that we may have "the peace of God, which passeth all understanding" (Philippians 4:7).

## Table 1. Criteria and Symptoms for Posttraumatic Stress Disorder (DSM-IV, 1994)

A. The person has been exposed to a traumatic event in which both of the following were present: (1) The person experienced, witnessed, or was confronted with an event or events that involved actual or threatened death or serious injury, or a threat to the physical integrity of self or others, (2) The person's response involved intense fear, helplessness or horror.

B. The traumatic event is persistently re-experienced in one (or more) of the following ways: (1) recurrent and intrusive distressing recollections of the event, including images, thoughts, or perceptions, (2) recurrent distressing dreams of the event, (3) acting or feeling as if the traumatic event were recurring, (4) intense psychological distress at exposure to internal or external cues that symbolize or resemble an aspect of the traumatic event, and (5) physiological reactivity on exposure to internal or external cues that symbolize . . . the event.

C. Persistent avoidance of stimuli associated with the trauma and numbing of general responsiveness as indicated by three or more of the following: (1) efforts to avoid thoughts, feelings, or conversations associated with the trauma, (2) efforts to avoid activities, places, or people that arouse recollections of the trauma, (3) inability to recall an important aspect of the trauma, (4) markedly diminished interest or participation in significant activities, (5) feeling of detachment or estrangement from others, (6) restricted range of affect (e.g., unable to have loving feelings), and (7) sense of a foreshortened future (does not expect to have a career, marriage, children, or a normal life span).

D. Persistent symptoms of increased arousal of the following: (1) difficulty falling or staying asleep, (2) irritability or outbursts of anger, (3) difficulty concentrating, etc.

## Table 2. Selecting a "Good-Enough" Therapist

A.  Three good reasons to find a therapist:
1.  You find yourself unable to cope with life.
2.  At least three people who matter to you have suggested it (even insisted).
3.  Everything you have tried, including sincere help from your ward, has not helped.

B.  Two ways to find a therapist who is right for you, always guided by prayer:
1.  Ask people you know and trust if they have a recommendation. Don't worry, the "stigma about being in therapy" has diminished. Most people realize that seeking psychological help for psychological distress is as necessary and smart as seeking medical help for physical problems.
2.  Check the rosters of state professional agencies: Marriage and Family Therapist Association, Psychological Association, American Medical Association, Association of Clinical Social Workers. And check to see if there is a branch of LDS Social Services near you.

C.  Four questions you have the right to ask your therapist:
1.  Are you licensed in the state in which you practice, and do you belong to professional organizations? (Diplomas and licenses should be posted.)
2.  What are your fees? Will you utilize my insurance? If I don't have insurance, would you be willing to bill my bishop? (Many wards are willing to help out for a short time.)
3.  What is your theory of how people change, and what interventions will you use?
4.  What do you think about the Mormon religion? (Good therapists do not necessarily have to share your belief system, but they do need to respect it.)

# Notes

Sally H. Barlow has been a member of the Brigham Young University psychology faculty for over twenty years. Since earning a Ph.D. from the University of Utah in 1978, she has served in a number of professional organizations, including as chair of the Utah Psychology Licensing Board, member-at-large for Division 49 of the American Psychological Association, and a Fellow of the Academy of Clinical Psychology. She earned a clinical diplomate from the American Board of Professional Psychologists, and is one of the first to receive a group diplomate from the American Board of Group Psychology. She has co-authored a book on family enrichment and has published chapters and articles on groups, women, and mental health and Mormons. Sally has held a number of positions in her ward, including Relief Society teacher and Laurel advisor, and is currently teaching the Gospel Doctrine class in the Corner Canyon Seventh Ward in Draper, Utah. Her son, Jack, is serving a mission in Cali, Colombia.

1. See Janice D. Yoder, *Women and Gender: Transforming Psychology* (New Jersey: Prentice Hall, 1999), p. 106.
2. Neal A. Maxwell, "From Whom All Blessings Flow," *Ensign*, 1997, p. 12.
3. *Webster's New Universal Unabridged Dictionary* (New York: Barnes and Noble Books, 1996), p. 2191.
4. See Petra Aarts and Wybrand Op den Velde, "Prior Traumatization and the Process of Aging: Theory and Clinical Implications," in Bessel Van der Kolk, Alexander McFarlane, and Lars Weisaeth, eds., *Traumatic Stress: The Effects of Overwhelming Experience on Mind, Body, and Society* (New York: Guilford Press, 1996), p. 368.
5. Conundrum Communication (Internet), Thursday, August 26, 1999, Behavioral Healthcare Bulletin 08.27.99, *dvaldez@consultnews.com*.
6. See Aarts and Op den Velde, "Prior Traumatization," p. 372.
7. See Judith Herman, *Trauma and Recovery: The Aftermath of Violence—from Domestic Abuse to Political Terror* (New York: Basic Books, 1992); Van der Kolk, McFarlane, and Weisaeth, *Traumatic Stress*.
8. See C. Clayton, S. Barlow, and B. Ballif-Spanvill, "Societal Groups and Aggression," in H. Hall, ed., *Lethal Violence: Effective Strategies for Assessing and Intervening in Fatal Group and Institutional Violence* (London: CRC Press, 1999), pp. 277–312.
9. See Aarts and Op den Velde, "Prior Traumatization."
10. Ibid., p. 372.
11. *Teachings of the Prophet Joseph Smith*, sel. Joseph Fielding Smith (Salt Lake City: Deseret Book, 1976), p. 255.
12. See Diane L. Spangler and David Burns, "Are Dysfunctional Attitudes and

Attributional Style the Same or Different?" *Behavior Therapy,* vol. 30, no. 2 (Spring 1999), pp. 239–52.

13. See David Burns, *Ten Days to Self-Esteem* (New York: William Morrow, 1993).

14. Gordon B. Hinckley, "Of You It Is Required to Forgive," *Ensign,* June 1991, p. 5.

15. Neal A. Maxwell, *Things As They Really Are* (Salt Lake City: Deseret Book, 1978), p. 119.

16. Dallin H. Oaks, " 'Judge Not' and Judging," *Ensign,* August 1999, p. 13.

17. See Suzanne R. Freedman and Robert D. Enright, "Forgiveness as an Intervention Goal with Incest Survivors," *Journal of Consulting and Clinical Psychology,* vol. 64, no. 5 (1996), pp. 983–92.

18. Maxwell, *Things As They Really Are,* p. 119; italics in original.

19. For further information about this, see Sally H. Barlow and Allen E. Bergin, "Religion and Mental Health from the Mormon Perspective," in H. G. Koenig, ed., *Handbook of Religion and Mental Health* (San Diego: Academic Press, 1998), pp. 225–43.

*Chapter 6*

# Evolution of the Mind, the Heart, and the Soul

**MARILYN S. BATEMAN**

*"Ye must grow in grace and in the knowledge of the truth"*
*D&C 50:40*

In February 1996, Sister Marjorie Hinckley, wife of the prophet, was selected by the Brigham Young University student leaders to receive the Exemplary Womanhood Award.

This award is given biennially by the Brigham Young University student body to honor a woman whose life exemplifies the teachings of the Lord and Savior, Jesus Christ. Upon receiving the award, Sister Hinckley responded by saying, "Anyone who has been active in the Church all her life has been made by the Church. The Church has made me what I am." Sister Hinckley's life reflects all that the gospel of Jesus Christ teaches. She has always been a believer in the truthfulness of the gospel. She has been not only an extraordinary companion to a key Church leader for many years but also a faithful mother and companion to her children. She has lived what she believes.

Ultimately, any person who seeks truth will be led to the gospel of Jesus Christ, for it contains all truth. Gospel principles bless all who seek to understand God's ways and his plan for the everlasting salvation of his children. The gospel teaches people who they are and the potential that life promises not only on this earth but also in the eternities. The teachings of the Lord Jesus Christ provide a clear understanding of mankind's relationship to God. Seekers after truth learn that they are his spirit children, that he is a loving and kind Father in Heaven and that each person's destiny is to return to a heavenly home if he or she will be true and faithful.

# Eternal Progress

In a survey of Americans performed for the Lutheran Brotherhood by Yankelovich Partners, most adults were concerned with and wanted answers to eternal questions. Those participating in the survey were asked the following question: "What [would you] ask a god or supreme being if [you] could get a direct and immediate answer?" The most frequently asked question was: "What's my purpose here?" Thirty-four percent, or more than one of every three persons, wanted to know the purpose of life. The second most popular question was: "Will I have life after death?" Almost one out of five persons asked that question. Another sixteen percent asked the question: "Why do bad things happen?" and another seven percent wondered if there is intelligent life elsewhere. Seventy-six percent of the individuals surveyed asked questions pertaining to one's ultimate purpose and eternity.[1] There is a thirst for spiritual knowledge. The answers to these questions are contained in the gospel of Jesus Christ. The plan of salvation as contained in the restored gospel provides clear and definitive answers to these queries.

The plan of salvation teaches that mortality is but one stage of life and that life existed before one's birth and stretches into the eternities after death. Life's purpose is to be "added upon," to be tested, to participate in a growth process that has eternal consequences. The knowledge gained and the decisions made in this life are critical and determine one's ultimate destiny. Mortality is a time to acquire spiritual knowledge, to be tested with respect to one's use of agency, to experience the bitter and the sweet, to learn from one's mistakes, and to succeed with the Lord's help. All of God's children are endowed with a special light or conscience which allows them to differentiate between truth and error (see John 1:9; Moroni 7:15–16) and to learn from experience. The more obedient one is to light, the more truth one receives (see D&C 50:24). It follows that the more consistent one's life is in living truth, the greater one's capacity and strength. Some individuals live in a time or place where access to truth is limited. Since earth life is but one phase in eternity, they will be given opportunities later (the millennium) consistent with their willingness to live whatever truths they enjoyed on earth (see D&C 137:5–10). There is life after death. There is intelligent life elsewhere (see Moses 1:33). There is purpose to life.

One of the most glorious truths contained in the Lord's plan is that of eternal progress—the opportunity to progress from mortality to immortality, to overcome death and receive a glorified resurrected body, to overcome weakness and to progress until one receives a glory and station like that of our eternal parents (see 1 Corinthians 15:42–44; D&C 76:94–95). President Gordon B. Hinckley has commented on this subject as follows: "The whole design of the gospel is to lead us, onward and upward to greater achievement, even, eventually, to godhood. This great possibility was enunciated by the Prophet Joseph Smith in the King Follet sermon . . . and emphasized by President Lorenzo Snow. It is this grand and incomparable concept: *As God now is, man may become!*"[2]

What is eternal progress? For those in mortality and the spirit world, it is an increase in spiritual knowledge, moral strength, and intelligence based on righteous living. It is the internalizing of true principles in the way one thinks and lives. It is repenting of one's sins and feeling the forgiveness that comes from the Atonement through the Holy Spirit. The scriptures indicate that intelligence is more than intellectual capacity. It is a righteous disposition that leads one to forsake evil (see D&C 93:36–37). The acquiring of spiritual knowledge and intelligence comes through diligence in obeying eternal laws. For one to receive the strength required to progress eternally, one must have a testimony that certain principles are true, a confirmation through the Holy Spirit that one is on the right path. This requires the companionship of the Holy Ghost. He serves as a teacher, a cleanser, a witness, a sanctifier, and a sealer. He links individuals into the power and grace of the Savior's atonement.

The growth process is characterized by small steps, as indicated by the Lord's words to Nephi: "For behold, thus saith the Lord God: I will give unto the children of men line upon line, precept upon precept, here a little and there a little; and blessed are those who hearken unto my precepts, and lend an ear unto my counsel, for they shall learn wisdom; for unto him that receiveth I will give more; and from them that shall say, We have enough, from them shall be taken away even that which they have" (2 Nephi 28:30).

The process of spiritual growth described in the above scripture is like a child learning to play the piano. The child begins with simple melodies that are mastered with hours of practice. The practice and lessons learned then provide the foundation for mastering more complex compositions. Eventually, with discipline and rigor and many additional practice hours over a significant period of time, an accomplished pianist is produced. Most growth processes in life are a type and shadow of the way in which God intends for us to grow, line upon line and precept upon precept, until we become finished products. President Hinckley has commented on the growth process in these words: "None of us . . . knows enough. The learning process is an endless process. We must read, we must observe, we must assimilate, and we must ponder that to which we expose our minds. I believe in evolution, not organic evolution, as it is called, but in the evolution of the mind, the heart, and the soul of man . . . I believe in growth."[3]

Several years ago, while my husband and I were living in Japan, we had the opportunity to visit the town of Wajima on the west coast. Wajima is the home of Japan's famous lacquerware. The Wajima factory has a display of the manufacturing process that illustrates the many steps required to create a beautiful piece of lacquerware. There are nineteen steps involved before the final design is added. Of particular interest is the number of times an item is polished following the additions of lacquer and lacquer paste. As I studied the various steps, I thought how like life the lacquerware manufacturing process is. As human beings, we are continually being added upon—growing from one lesson to another, from grace to grace.

Polishing is part of life. Polishing removes the rough edges. Often, polishing is represented by the hard times, the difficult times, the sad times. God does not inflict evil upon us or pave our way with stones. The "bad times" referred to in the Yankelovich survey are often man-made or environmental in origin. Even so, they are part of the design of life. Their purpose is to burnish our souls and help us understand our dependence on God. When we are exhausted from the trials of the day, the Lord through his Spirit refreshes our spirit and prepares us for a new day. Our purpose is not to escape problems but to overcome them with the Lord's help. God through his prophets said, "I have refined thee, but not with silver; I have chosen thee in the furnace of affliction" (Isaiah 48:10), and "that all these things shall give thee experience, and shall be for thy good" (D&C 122:7). The heat of the day may not only exhaust us but also purge the impurities within.

In Matthew 5:48 the Lord admonishes all of us: "Be ye therefore perfect, even as your Father which is in heaven is perfect." It is possible in the eternities to know all things and have the capacity to endure all things and live according to all truth. However, the goal will not be reached in this lifetime, nor can it be accomplished on one's own. As imperfect beings subject to the world's temptations we need the help of an all-wise Father and his Son. We can only be perfected through the Father's plan, with the core of that plan centered in Christ and his atonement (see Moroni 10:32–33).

During the time we lived in Japan we were provided a furnished apartment. Consequently there were only a few items that we took with us from our home in the United States. Family pictures, books, favorite recipes, and a beautiful crystal egg were among the items. At one point in time the crystal egg belonged to our daughter Michele. It had been part of her egg collection. When Michele married, she took the eggs to her new home with the exception of the one made of crystal. She said to me, "You keep it, Mom. I know how much you admire it." The crystal egg was special to me. First, it reminded me of Michele, her generosity, her purity, and her desire to serve others. It reminded me of the many other eggs in Michele's collection. As the egg collection grew over a number of years, I often thought how like people they are—some large, some small, some plain, others decorative and colorful. Some of the eggs were humorous and others dignified. Looking at the eggs was like looking at humanity—each special in its uniqueness.

The crystal egg also reminds me of perfection. It has many facets. When the egg is held up to the light, the crystal facets seem to attract, cleave to, and then reflect the light rays. It sets a standard for me. I would like to attract the light of truth into my life and then reflect light to others. I desire to be a servant of Jesus Christ and reflect his light. If the world were filled with light, it would be perfect—perfect in Christ. We would have experienced the step-by-step process of having been born of God. We would have the image of Christ in our countenances (see Alma 5:14).

## Grace: The Power to Grow, to Forgive, and to Lift

What is the process by which one becomes perfect? What is grace? How do we partake of the grace offered by the Father and the Son? What does it mean to grow from grace to grace? What is the role of the Holy Ghost in the growth process? Is he more than a prompter? How does he link us to the blessings of grace?

Grace is defined as a "divine means of help or strength, given through the bounteous mercy and love of Jesus Christ." It is also described as "an enabling power that allows men and women to lay hold on eternal life and exaltation after they have expended their own best efforts" (Bible Dictionary, p. 697). Thus, the scripture states: "It is by grace that we are saved, after all we can do" (2 Nephi 25:23). During an appearance of the Savior to his Apostles following the resurrection, he said, "All power is given unto me in heaven and in earth" (Matthew 28:18). Through the Atonement, the Savior not only paid the price for sin but also experienced the pains, sufferings, temptations, sicknesses, and infirmities of every person in order that he would know "according to the flesh how to succor his people" (Alma 7:11–12). For those weighed down by sin, he knows how to heal. For those exhausted by the burdens of everyday living, he knows how to lift.

Our daughter Michele and her husband are experiencing the trauma of helping their oldest son, Douglas, cope with the challenges of leukemia. Shortly after the diagnosis was made, doctors assured the young boy and his parents that the probability of remission was near 80 percent if the prescribed therapy was strictly followed. Over a period of three and one-half years, Douglas endured the chemotherapy and other medicines administered. Finally, the day came when the doctors pronounced him in remission. A checkup was scheduled for the following month. Thirty days later the tests revealed that the disease had returned. It was not in remission. The medicines had controlled the leukemia but not eliminated it from his system. More chemotherapy was prescribed and preparation for a bone marrow transplant was recommended.

At this point in time the outcome is unknown. Parents and son plus brothers and sister are learning to take one day at a time. As a grandparent, my prayers have become more fervent and frequent. There have been pleadings asking that the doctors will know what to do and that this family will be blessed with peace, comfort, and hope. One wonders what a fourteen-year-old boy thinks about after four years of partial confinement and weekly doses of poison. The saving element has been an understanding of the Lord's plan of salvation— for both parents and son. Peace has come through the Comforter and, although the daily task of facing the unknown is arduous, there is a calmness and hope in knowing that mortality is a moment in eternity. The Lord's grace has been extended to this family. An enabling power has entered their lives to lift them up and assure them of an eternal relationship.

During his mortal ministry Jesus indicated that a person must be linked to him in order to receive the blessings of the atoning sacrifice. He said: "I am the true vine, and my Father is the husbandman. Every branch in me that beareth not fruit he taketh away: and every branch that beareth fruit, he purgeth it, that it may bring forth more fruit. . . . Abide in me, and I in you. As the branch cannot bear fruit of itself, except it abide in the vine; no more can ye, except ye abide in me" (John 15:1–2, 4).

The scripture indicates that all of us must come to Christ in order to produce good fruit, in order to receive the comfort and hope required to face adversity, in order to receive forgiveness for sin. Moroni further states that we are "perfected in him" if we deny ourselves of all ungodliness. If we love God "with all [our] might, mind and strength, then is his grace sufficient for [us], that by his grace [we] may be perfect in Christ" (Moroni 10:32).

How does one become a branch attached to the vine? How does one come to Christ and "lay hold upon every good gift" (Moroni 10:30)? The answer is to participate in the ordinances and covenants of The Church of Jesus Christ of Latter-day Saints and to be obedient to the promises made. Notice that the fruitful branch in John 15 will be purged at times in order to become more fruitful. The path one treads will not be smooth.

The doctrine of grace is mentioned more than two hundred times in the scriptures. This enabling power is lovingly and mercifully given by Jesus Christ to assist us through the challenges of mortality. This power is activated by the principle of faith in the Savior, repentance, baptism, the gift of the Holy Ghost, and righteous living. We earn the right to access the power of grace and to grow "from grace to grace" when we seek to keep the commandments (D&C 93:13).

The story of Amanda Smith illustrates vividly the challenges and disappointments that may occur in life while at the same time portraying the grace offered by the Savior. Amanda was born in 1809 in Becket, Massachusetts. As a young girl she moved with her family to Ohio, where she became a member of the Campbellite faith. Along with Sidney Rigdon and others, she heard the restored gospel preached and joined the Church in 1831. She moved to Kirtland and assisted in the building of the temple. In 1838, she and her family were forced to leave Kirtland because of mob violence. They made their way by wagon to Caldwell County, Missouri. Two days before arriving they were accosted by an armed mob that demanded all their weapons and ammunition.

Upon arriving at Haun's Mill, her husband pitched a tent by the blacksmith's shop. As she sat in the tent resting from the journey she saw a mob coming—the same group of men that had taken their weapons earlier. The following is her description of the events that followed:

> Before I could get to the blacksmith's shop door to alarm the brethren, who were at prayers, the bullets were whistling amongst them. I seized my two little girls and escaped across the millpond on a slab-walk. . . . When the firing had ceased I went back to the scene of the massacre, for there were my husband and three sons, of whose fate I as yet knew nothing. . . .
>
> Emerging from the blacksmith shop was my eldest son, bearing on his shoulders his little brother Alma. "Oh! my Alma is dead!" I cried, in anguish. "No, Mother; I

think Alma is not dead. But Father and brother Sardius are killed!" What an answer was this to appall me! My husband and son murdered, another little son seemingly mortally wounded. . . .

But I could not weep then. The fountain of tears was dry; the heart overburdened with its calamity, and all the mother's sense absorbed in its anxiety for the precious boy which God alone could save by his miraculous aid. The entire hip joint of my wounded boy had been shot away. Flesh, hip bone, joint, and all had been ploughed out from the muzzle of the gun which the ruffian placed to the child's hip through the logs of the shop and deliberately fired. We laid little Alma on a bed in our tent and I examined the wound. It was a ghastly sight. I knew not what to do. It was night now. . . . women were sobbing, in the greatest anguish of spirit; the children were crying loudly with fear and grief at the loss of fathers and brothers. . . . Yet was I there all that long, dreadful night, with my dead and my wounded, and none but God as our physician and help. "Oh, my Heavenly Father," I cried, "what shall I do? Thou seest my poor wounded boy and knowest my inexperience. Oh, Heavenly Father direct me what to do!" And then I was directed as by a voice speaking to me.

The ashes of our fire was still smouldering. We had been burning the bark of the shag-bark hickory. I was directed to take those ashes and make a lye and put a cloth saturated with it right into the wound. It hurt, but little Alma was too near dead to heed it much. Again and again I saturated the cloth and put it into the hole from which the hip joint had been ploughed, and each time mashed flesh and splinters of bone came away with the cloth, and the wound became as white as chicken's flesh. Having done as directed I again prayed to the Lord and was again instructed as distinctly as though a physician had been standing by speaking to me. Nearby was a slippery-elm tree. From this I was told to make a slippery-elm poultice and fill the wound with it. My eldest boy was sent to get the slippery-elm from the roots, the poultice was made, and the wound, which took fully a quarter of a yard of linen to cover, so large was it, was properly dressed. . . .

I removed the wounded boy to a house, some distance off, the next day, and dressed his hip, the Lord directing me as before. I was reminded that in my husband's trunk there was a bottle of balsam. This I poured into the wound, greatly soothing Alma's pain. "Alma, my child," I said, "you believe that the Lord made your hip?" "Yes, Mother." "Well, the Lord can make something there in the place of your hip, don't you believe he can, Alma?" "Do you think that the Lord can, Mother?" inquired the child, in his simplicity. "Yes, my son," I replied, "he has shown it all to me in a vision." Then I laid him comfortably on his face, and said: "Now you lie like that, and don't move, and the Lord will make you another hip."

So Alma lay on his face for five weeks, until he was entirely recovered—a flexible gristle having grown in place of the missing joint and socket, which remains to this day a marvel to physicians. On the day that he walked again I was out of the house fetching a bucket of water when I heard screams from the children. Running back, in affright, I entered, and there was Alma on the floor, dancing around, and the children screaming in astonishment and joy. It is now nearly forty years ago, but Alma has never been the least crippled during his life, and he has traveled quite a long period of the time as a missionary of the gospel and a living miracle of the power of God.[4]

The Prophet Joseph Smith was shown the record of John the Baptist in which John "saw that [Jesus] received not of the fulness at the first, but received grace for grace; and he received not of the fulness at first, but continued from grace to grace, until he received a fulness" (D&C 93:12–13). This passage describes the growth process. As Jesus served and blessed others, his enabling power was increased until he received a fulness. The Lord continues to extend grace to his faithful brothers and sisters as they bless others. Amanda Smith's faith was sufficient to be taught by the Holy Ghost what she could do to save her son's life and hip. Her thoughts were not for herself, but for her boy. Her service to him coupled with her faith and worthiness brought knowledge and peace to her and relief to her son.

Just as Jesus received grace for grace and grew from grace to grace, so the growth process is the same for us. The Lord told the Prophet Joseph: "For if you keep my commandments you shall receive of his fulness, and be glorified in me as I am in the Father; therefore, I say unto you, you shall receive grace for grace" (D&C 93:20).

A short time ago one of our neighbors was in a car accident. The driver of the other car, a recent immigrant, was at fault. Police were called to the scene, information was exchanged, and the neighbor learned that the person who caused the accident did not have insurance. However, the immigrant promised to pay for the damage.

When my neighbor's car was repaired, he took the bill to the home of the other driver. The damage was more extensive than initial appraisals had forecast, and the bill was well beyond anything either driver had expected. As the neighbor saw the facial expression of the immigrant, it was apparent that the man did not have the financial capacity to meet the obligation. The immigrant finally said, "Perhaps I can take out a loan." My neighbor, realizing that his own personal finances were significantly better than those of his new friend, said, "No! I will take care of the bill. But could you help me? I have need of someone to take care of my home for a week while I take my family on vacation. Are you in a position to help me?" The answer was an immediate "yes." What a wonderful solution! Whether the exchanges were equal or not did not matter. My neighbor could pay the bill and the other person could give of his time in return. Grace was exchanged for grace.

## Summary

We worship God through the service we render others combined with obedience to eternal principles and ordinances. There are many ways to gain and share gospel learning. One way is through formal study. The Lord has commanded us to "seek . . . out of the best books words of wisdom; seek learning, even by study and also by faith" (D&C 88:118). Earlier in the same section, we are told to become "instructed. . . in theory, in principle, in doctrine, in the law of the gospel. . . Of things both in heaven and in the earth, and under the earth; things which have been, things which are, things which must shortly come to pass" (D&C 88:78–79). As President Hinckley stated, there are so many things to learn and such a short time in which to learn them.

The purpose of our learning effort is eternal in nature. Secular learning is important, as noted in the eighty-eighth section of the Doctrine and Covenants. But there is a danger when one takes pride in one's scholarship, when one does not couple scholarship with discipleship. Nephi, speaking of the last days, said that "priests shall contend one with another, and they shall *teach with their learning,* and deny the Holy Ghost, which giveth utterance" (2 Nephi 28:4; emphasis added). Some truths are more important than others. President Spencer W. Kimball stated plainly: "The secular without the foundation of the spiritual is but like the foam upon the milk, the fleeting shadow."[5] Sacred truths are key to one's eternal progress. Paul told Timothy that the last days would be perilous times because "men shall be lovers of their own selves. . . Having a form of godliness, but denying the power thereof. . . Ever learning, and never able to come to the knowledge of the truth" (2 Timothy 3:1–7).

Another form of learning is daily experience. Trials and tribulations teach some of life's great lessons. Michele's family will never be the same. The truths learned about eternal relationships are not found in reading books. They are learned in God's "furnace of affliction."

Living worthy of the companionship of the Holy Ghost is indispensable to internalizing spiritual truth. He is the member of the Godhead with the responsibility to "teach [us] all things, to bring all things to [our] remembrance," to "show [us] things to come" (John 14:26; 16:13). He is the one that links us to Christ by touching our lives with the powers and grace of the Atonement. The atoning sacrifice of the Lord Jesus Christ is the foundation for eternal progress. The sacrifice in the garden and on the cross is the instrument that opens the door to spiritual growth. Christ's power to cleanse and sanctify emanating from the Atonement allows us to change over time as we prove faithful to covenants and ordinances. If we come to him, he turns us into new creatures (see 2 Corinthians 5:17). He has the power to infuse divine attributes in the faithful over time and each day. These attributes or characteristics are also known as the fruits of the Spirit (see 2 Peter 1:4–8; Galatians 5:22–23). The Holy Ghost is the means by which we receive them.

"Behold, ye are little children and ye cannot bear all things now; ye must grow in grace and in the knowledge of the truth. Fear not, little children, for you are mine, and I have overcome the world, and you are of them that my Father hath given me" (D&C 50:40–41).

# Notes

Marilyn S. Bateman is the wife of Brigham Young University President Merrill S. Bateman. She is the mother of seven children and grandmother of twenty-four. She has traveled to and lived in such diverse places as England, Japan, and Jakarta.

1. "USA Snapshots," *USA*, June 1, 1999.
2. *Teachings of Gordon B. Hinckley* (Salt Lake City: Deseret Book, 1997), p. 179; italics in original.
3. Ibid., p. 298.
4. Leon R. Hartshorn, comp., *Remarkable Stories from the Lives of Latter-day Saint Women* (Salt Lake City: Deseret Book, 1973), pp. 164–67.
5. *The Teachings of Spencer W. Kimball*, ed. Edward L. Kimball (Salt Lake City: Bookcraft, 1982), p. 390.

*Chapter 7*

# The Crowning Blessing of the Church

**COLLEEN W. ASAY**

*"Temples and the performance of ordinances therein"*
*D&C 138:54*

On a quiet evening in April 1999 my husband's heart stopped beating, resulting in "sudden death." The immediate coma persisted for five days—his body not willing to give up the spirit that gave it life. During those days our family experienced the presence of the Holy Spirit more fully than we had known before.

Speaking in the memorial service, President Boyd K. Packer, Acting President of the Quorum of the Twelve, with his phenomenal spiritual insight, assured me that my husband's stepping through the veil would be spiritually rejuvenating, even though a happy/sad occurrence. He then reminded me that the blessing I had of serving in the Salt Lake Temple would help me understand death in a way that I could not otherwise know. The ensuing days have borne out the truth of his comforting words.

Understanding death as an essential part of our existence did come to me while acting as matron of the Salt Lake Temple. My eyes were opened and my soul expanded as I learned the possibilities inherent in the plan of salvation. I perceived more fully Jacob's testament that "death hath passed upon all men, to fulfil the merciful plan of the great Creator" (2 Nephi 9:6). Moreover, I learned of many essential personal blessings available to each of our Heavenly Father's children while living in mortality; blessings that are available only in God's Holy House—the temple. I do, therefore, draw your attention to the importance of the temple and the blessings and personal applications of the vital ordinances performed therein.

## The Temple—A House of God

The history of building temples in this dispensation began with continual challenges. From modern-day revelation we learn that Joseph Smith was commanded early in the Restoration to build a temple. This was not easy. The early

Saints were an impoverished people barely able to sustain themselves. They sacrificed their means, time, and energies to comply with the command of the Lord. Men would donate one day of ten to work on the Lord's House. Women donated their fine china to be crushed and mixed with the plaster to give a luster to the temple walls. The sisters also made clothing for the workmen and provided food for them as they worked. When the already indignant local populace saw the Saints' feverish efforts in building such a magnificent edifice and learned why the structure was so important their anger against them became even more threatening. It soon became necessary for the brethren to work with a tool in one hand and a protective weapon at their sides to safeguard themselves and to prevent the growing building from being destroyed.

The first temple, built in Kirtland, Ohio, was used for several years, but had to be abandoned when the Saints were forced from the area. Later when the Saints were gathered together in Nauvoo, Illinois, they commenced a temple and worked on it in feverish haste. The Saints knew all the while they would not be free to use it. Edicts enforced by enraged local citizens soon required them, under threat of death, to vacate the whole area. After the mob had desecrated the sacred edifice in several ways, in October 1848 an incendiary set fire to the temple and burned it down.

Just four days after arriving in the Salt Lake Valley Brigham Young selected a site for a temple. Even though they were far from their persecutors, the challenges of building homes and farms and businesses often slowed the work on the temple. A major threat to the work was occasioned by the arrival of federal troops to occupy part of the Utah Territory.

So that their efforts thus far would not be discovered and the foundation work of the temple perhaps be destroyed, they hid that work under piles of earth and debris.

The Saints have always been resolute in their efforts to build houses to the Lord in spite of harassment. Why in the face of all this opposition have they persisted? Because the Lord promised that "in the which house I design to endow those whom I have chosen with power from on high" (D&C 95:8). He also wanted to have a place "that the Son of Man might . . . manifest himself to his people" (D&C 109:5). "That he may . . . restore again that which was lost or which he hath taken away, even the fulness of the priesthood" (D&C 124:28).

There are many beautiful places of worship throughout the world, including cathedrals, synagogues, mosques, churches, and monasteries. However, there is only one place where one can feel the power, influence, and inspiration of the Son of Man. There is only one place where the Spirit constrains one to acknowledge His House is "a place of . . . holiness" (D&C 109:13). The temples of the Lord have something to give that can be obtained in no other place.[1]

## Crowning Blessings of Temple Worship

After visiting Temple Square in Salt Lake City, a young man, his wife, and their three children approached the main foyer of the Salt Lake Temple. The father said to the attendant there: "We have just finished a tour on Temple Square. Our guide told us that in this building husbands and wives can be married for time and eternity and with their children become a forever family. We want to participate in that service!"

The bewildered attendant asked for the young man's

temple recommend, only to find out that he was not a member of the Church. The man persisted in his request to have his family united to him forever to the point of becoming belligerent and had to be escorted from the temple by several security men—followed by his weeping wife and children.

They were not the only ones crying, however. Those who had witnessed this scene were visibly touched. As I watched the event, President Spencer W. Kimball's declaration to the youth of the Church flashed into my mind: "If you understood the ordinances of the House of the Lord, you would crawl on your hands and feet for thousands of miles in order to receive them!"[2] I was comforted in knowing that the blessings of the temple are available to any worthy member, and I knew that this young family also could take the necessary steps to someday claim the glorifying blessing of temple worship that they were seeking.

There is, however, a more serious concern, and that is for those who are worthy members of the Church who deliberately deny themselves the crowning blessings of the restored gospel.

## *Deny Not Yourself the Blessings of the Temple*

Some years ago our family moved into a new ward. One of the first sisters to introduce herself was Ann. Ann was serving in the Primary when I first met her, and later she was called to serve in the Young Women organization. I admired her willingness to give freely of her time in Church callings.

She and her husband were both very committed and active in the ward. They appeared to live the gospel in every way.

When I became her visiting teacher, I was surprised to learn that Ann and her husband had never been to the temple. This puzzled me. I asked Ann on one visit if there were some problem that prevented temple attendance. She said, "Yes, me." To my astonishment she said that she was not worthy of going to the temple because she was not yet perfect in keeping the commandments. Ann said she knew of the commitments made in temples and until she felt she could live in accord with what was required, she could not in good conscience go to the temple.

Her response puzzled and worried me. At that time I did not know how to respond to her. We soon moved from that area, but I did not forget about Ann. Since serving in the temple I have pondered often about my dear friend. I have frequently wished I could tell her what I now know about the temple. I would bear my fervent testimony that the crowning blessing of the Lord's gospel is temple worship.

## "We Must Do So Little to Receive So Much"

Our finite minds cannot comprehend the magnitude of the blessings available to us today. To gain a deeper appreciation of the temple, you may want to try the following: Michael Wilcox, an instructor at the Institute of Religion at the University of Utah, writes that he often asks his students to write a paper on the 109th section of the Doctrine and Covenants, which is the dedicatory prayer for the Kirtland

Temple. Their assignment is to identify every blessing in the prayer that comes to the Saints from temple worship. After completing the list, they are to identify every word or phrase that suggests what they must do to receive those blessings. He writes: "Their papers are wonderful to read, and I have received many insights from them, but one paper in particular struck me. After listing the blessings she had found and how to receive them, one young lady concluded her paper with these words: 'I think it is significant and revealing of the Lord's character that we must do so little to be able to receive so much.' "[3]

I encourage you to take a few minutes and follow Brother Wilcox's suggestion. I did and was astonished at the number of key blessings I discovered in that dedicatory prayer. It is indeed "significant and revealing of the Lord's character that we must do so little to be able to receive so much." To all, including the Anns of the Church, I promise this brief exercise will increase your appreciation of the temple service and create within you a desire to make the temple part of your lives.

## Key Blessings of the Temple

There are those who have never gained an understanding of temples and temple ordinances; thus, they turn their backs to the place that offers a wealth of precious truths, unlimited blessings, and the prospects of abiding happiness. Perhaps it would help some people hold the temple in higher esteem and cause them to seek its blessings with greater intent and consistency, if their views were expanded to include the following:

1. *The blessings of an examined life.* Only certified members

are permitted to enter the House of the Lord. Such certification comes through searching interviews with priesthood leaders annually and the issuance of temple recommends.

This process provides us an opportunity to examine and prove ourselves, whether we be in the faith (see 2 Corinthians 13:5). It involves a review of our lives with ordained servants of the Lord who can help us correct anything that is amiss.

A few years ago my sister Karen made an appointment with her bishop for a temple recommend interview. On the appointed date she went to the bishop's office, answered the prescribed questions, received her recommend, and was told to obtain a second signature from a member of the stake presidency.

When Karen arrived at the stake offices she was met by a very conscientious member of the stake presidency. She was invited to sit down. He took the time to get acquainted. He asked all of the required questions and emphasized the importance of worshipping in the House of the Lord frequently. At the close of the conversation he looked earnestly into Karen's eyes and asked, "How many years has it been since you obtained your first temple recommend?"

Karen reflected a moment and answered, "Almost twenty-five years."

Pausing briefly and allowing Karen to mull over her response, the president continued, "Are you twenty-five times better today than you were then?"

The thought-provoking inquiry caused Karen to do some serious soul-searching. She could not dismiss from her mind the words of her concerned priesthood leader. Over and over again she wondered, "Am I progressing in my life as I should be progressing? Do I serve in my Church calling with a singleness of purpose? Am I walking so as to keep myself blameless before God?" (see Alma 5:27).

The warning words of Socrates say, "An unexamined life is not worth living." How blessed we are to belong to a church with temples and a program requiring annual examinations of our lives!

2. *The blessings of being perfected in an understanding of our ministries.* In section 97 of the Doctrine and Covenants, reference is made to the temple as "a place of instruction for all those who are called to the work of the ministry in all their several callings and offices; that they may be perfected in the understanding of their ministry" (vv. 13–14). Exactly what is a woman's ministry? In the temple the role of a woman is clearly defined by our Father in Heaven. That role was given to Eve in the Garden of Eden. This divinely given distinction is largely ignored by women of today. The significance associated with the divine designation "helpmeet" is lost in a self-aggrandizing world.

In the temple women learn from divine laws and patterns. For example, it is in the temple we are taught the kind of homes we should have. It is not happenstance that the Lord revealed to Joseph Smith that His House should be a "house of order" and that it should be a house of prayer, of fasting, of faith, of learning, and of glory (D&C 109:8). This House of God was to be for us the celestial pattern to be simulated by his children in their earthly homes; a celestial pattern to dominate and reign in our earthly telestial home so that our children will feel "at home" when they return to their Heavenly Father in his celestial home.

It is in the temple that the words from the hymn "O My Father" (*Hymns*, no. 292) take on new meaning. Borrowing words from that beloved song, it is in the temple that we regain our Father's presence (or feel the manifestation of his spirit.) It is in the temple we learn that in his holy habitation our spirits once did reside, and in that primeval childhood we were nurtured near his side. In the temple we learn of his wise and glorious purpose, and in the temple we feel a secret something whispering, You're *not* a stranger here. It is in the temple we realize that we have wandered into a more exalted sphere and recognize the sweet, familiar aura associated with our former home. It has been said by many of our leaders that the temple is heaven on earth—as our homes can become.

I am convinced that the influence of women upon their husbands and children would be enhanced significantly if while under the influence of the divine tutelage of the temple they would seek an understanding of their ministry in the home.

3. *The blessing of being on the bridge spanning heaven and earth or linking the land of the living with the land of the dead.* Thornton Niven Wilder wrote, "There is a land of the living and a land of the dead and the bridge is love."[4] I often heard my husband say, "There is a land of the living and a land of the dead, and the bridge between is the holy temple where the labor of love is performed."

On this bridge mortals reach out to those who have gone before and do things for them that they cannot do for themselves. By performing this labor of love, Latter-day Saints become saviors on Mount Zion and draw closer to the Savior of all mankind (see Obadiah 1:21).

On this bridge, saving and exalting ordinances are performed in the presence of God, angels, and living witnesses.

And it is on this bridge that ordinances are performed that pertain to both time and eternity.

A short time ago a family group gathered in the celestial room. A member of the temple presidency welcomed them and quietly inquired about the purpose for their visit. One man stepped forward and with a tear in his eye explained, "This afternoon we are burying our father. On his deathbed he made us promise that on the day of his burial we would all be in the temple where we might feel a closeness to him."

On another occasion a young couple with three children (one of whom was autistic) came to the temple to receive their endowment, be sealed as husband and wife, and have their children sealed to them. They were scheduled to be at the temple an hour and a half before the beginning of the live session. However, they were late in arriving. The young wife explained that her father had passed away during the night. They had postponed their temple blessings several times in hopes that the father would recover and be able to attend the temple with them. Now at his death they did not want to postpone it again. Imagine their joy as they entered the sealing room of the temple to find her mother and brothers and sisters seated there. After the ceremony the couple confirmed that the presence of her father they felt had made the occasion complete. They rejoiced knowing, as we knew, that the temple is the bridge between heaven and earth.

On the temple bridge the veil between the world of the living and the world of the dead is very thin, for this bridge spans the place where we now live and the place where we shall all go in due time.

# "I Will Manifest Myself There"

I have discussed just three significant blessings: (1) the blessing of an examined life, (2) the blessing of being perfected in an understanding of our ministries, and (3) the blessing of being on the bridge spanning heaven and earth. Many other blessings and personal applications related to the House of God could be cited. I have said little or nothing about

• the blessing of becoming better acquainted with God and realizing the promise of a manifestation of the Son of Man (see D&C 109:5);

• the blessing of engaging in true worship and practicing pure religion;

• the blessing of putting on the full armor of God (see Ephesians 6:13–18);

• the blessing of growing up in God, receiving a fulness of the Holy Ghost, becoming organized according to God's laws, and obtaining every needful thing (see D&C 109:15); or

• the blessing of being sealed to husbands and children and parents for time without end.

Let us not forget the sorrow of the family that could not partake of the blessing of being united forever. It is worth every price we must pay to be able to enter and involve ourselves in the blessings of the House of the Lord. Joseph Smith taught, "The main object [of gathering] was to build unto the Lord a house whereby He could reveal unto His people the ordinances of His house and the glories of His kingdom, and teach the people the way of salvation."[5]

Let us not make the mistake of Ann and others in thinking we have to be perfect in order to enter the temple. It is there that the "mysteries" of the kingdom are revealed to us which guide us to perfection. It is in the temple performing the ordinances there that "things which have been kept hid from before the foundation of the world" are revealed (D&C 124:39, 41).

I testify that the temple and the ordinances performed there are all that I have said and more—much more! God bless us to appreciate this wonderful place. May we receive its sanctifying influence and blessings.

## *Notes*

Colleen W. Asay is a member of the Moss Hill Ward in Bountiful, Utah. She is currently serving as stake Relief Society president in the Salt Lake University First Stake. Prior to that she served for two and a half years with her husband in the Salt Lake Temple, where she was temple matron. She was born and reared in Monroe, Utah. She married Carlos E. Asay, and they have eight children and thirty-six grandchildren.

1. See Boyd K. Packer, *The Holy Temple* (Salt Lake City: Bookcraft, 1980), p. 11.
2. As quoted in *Temples of the Ancient World,* ed. Donald W. Parry (Salt Lake City: Deseret Book, 1994), pp. 58–59.
3. Michael Wilcox, *House of Glory* (Salt Lake City: Deseret Book, 1995), p. 67.
4. As quoted in John Bartlett, *Familiar Quotations,* 16th ed. (Boston: Little, Brown and Company, 1992), p. 697.
5. *Teachings of the Prophet Joseph Smith,* sel. Joseph Fielding Smith (Salt Lake City: Deseret Book, 1976), p. 308.

*Chapter 8*

# Genealogy: More Than Just a Nice Hobby

**BARBARA H. BAKER AND SANDRA S. PITTS**

*"Whatsoever you bind on earth, may be bound in heaven"*
*D&C 127:7*

Do you ever feel bored or in a rut, useless or unfulfilled, old or out of circulation, isolated or lonely? Maybe you need a pick-me-up, a boost, even an exciting hobby. We would like to suggest our hobby, and we think there is nothing better to pick you up or give you a boost. Pursuit of our hobby will make you feel like a detective and could turn you into a published author. Doesn't that sound exciting? With our hobby, you will never feel bored or useless, and you will be giving great service to millions as well as to your Father in Heaven. It doesn't take a lot of prior knowledge, expertise, or training, it just takes enthusiasm, persistence, and a loving, willing heart.

Have you guessed what our hobby is? It is family history research—genealogy. It is the hobby of young and old, male and female, but it is a hobby for which older women can have a very special affinity and gift.

If you should visit the Family History Library™ in Salt Lake City on any given day of the year, you are almost certain to encounter someone who is far from home. She could be from England or Australia, Germany or South Africa, France or South America, Scandinavia or the Orient, or any one of the fifty United States. Library patrons come to the Family History Library from all over the world to research their family history. Ofttimes they come as part of a tour group organized by a genealogical society in their home area and they stay for several days of intense family history research. At the end of each day, when the library closes, they leave reluctantly but mentally exhausted from a hard day's research.

If you were to chat with one of these library visitors, chances are you would learn that he or she—more likely she—is not a member of The Church of Jesus Christ of Latter-day Saints. You might wonder: What motivates such people to want to research their family history? It isn't a desire to do temple work for their ancestors. So, what drives them?

For many do feel driven. Some might say that they've

"caught the bug." Whether they know it or not, the Spirit of Elijah has touched their hearts. "The Prophet Elijah was to plant in the hearts of the children the promises made to their fathers, foreshadowing the great work to be done in the temples of the Lord in the dispensation of the fulness of times" (D&C 138:47–48).

The Lord is influencing nonmembers and placing them in positions to help further his work. Members of the Church have benefited immeasurably from the research nonmembers have done in pursuit of their ancestry, for whatever reason. Nonmembers who research their family histories help members by publishing their histories, forming family organizations, contributing to genealogical periodicals and newsletters, sharing their research through computer databases, working on indexing projects, and volunteering at over three thousand Family History Centers™ worldwide. Nonmembers may believe that genealogy is just a hobby, and it has been said that genealogical research without temple work is just that—a nice hobby. But members of the Church know differently. President Gordon B. Hinckley has said: "If temple ordinances are an essential part of the restored gospel, and I testify that they are, then we must provide the means by which they can be accomplished. All of our vast family history endeavor is directed to temple work. There is no other purpose for it. The temple ordinances become the crowning blessings the Church has to offer."[1]

If the Lord can influence those who are not yet members of his Church, then his influence on the members of his Church is far greater. If we as members do not take advantage of the assistance that the Lord provides for us, in part through nonmembers, it will be a terrible shame with eternal consequences. We need to open our hearts to the possibilities.

Locating records that will document events in the lives of our deceased ancestors is vital to their salvation and ours:

> And now, my dearly beloved brethren and sisters, let me assure you that these are principles in relation to the dead and the living that cannot be lightly passed over, as pertaining to our salvation. For their salvation is necessary and essential to our salvation, as Paul says concerning the fathers—that they without us cannot be made perfect—neither can we without our dead be made perfect. . . . It is sufficient to know, in this case, that the earth will be smitten with a curse unless there is a welding link of some kind or other between the fathers and the children, upon some subject or other—and behold what is that subject? It is the baptism for the dead. (D&C 128:15, 18)

The Lord does not leave us alone to accomplish this sometimes very difficult task. When we have done all we can do, he will help us. The Spirit is especially strong at the Family History Library. Little "miracles" take place every day that bear witness of the divine nature of this work. The librarians and missionaries who work in the Library and in Family History Centers are frequent witnesses to these events. We would like to share some of them with you:

A non-LDS woman from Seattle came to the Family History Library to do some research for a friend who could not travel. She approached a British Reference Consultant and asked for help to find information on Sir John Henry Coode. It was discovered in a book of British biographies that he was born in Cornwall, England, in 1779 and died in 1858. With the newly found death date, the consultant asked the patron if she had looked for a will for Sir John Coode, explaining that he would probably have left one. Her answer was "no," so the consultant showed her how to find his will.

After a while the consultant felt impressed to go look for the patron in the microfilm readers to see if she was having success. As she approached the patron she asked, "Did you find the will of John Coode?" Before she could answer, another woman sitting in the same row of readers immediately turned and asked, "Did you say John Coode?" The second patron, also a visitor from out of town, was searching for information about Sir John Henry Coode. She had a copy of his will in front of her! If that weren't enough of a coincidence, both of the out-of-towners were staying at the same bed-and-breakfast, and they spent the evening together comparing and sharing their findings.

Another instance occurred that helped a Library Reference Consultant with her own family work. Her mother was one of nine children in an LDS family, born and raised in Salt Lake City. She had recently passed away at age seventy-nine. The daughter began to wonder if her mother's only living sibling, an older brother named Richard Squire (not his real name), a resident of Idaho, was still alive. He and his family had not been active in the Church over the years, and he hadn't been at his sister's funeral. If he had died, then he would need to have some of his temple ordinances completed.

The consultant was partway into a two-hour shift at the reference desk one day when an older lady came to her and asked for help to use a new computer research tool, the Social Security Death Index. She went with the lady to the computer, where the woman's son was trying to use the Index.

The consultant asked who they were trying to find. They said, "Richard Squire."

A bit stunned, she asked, "Which Richard Squire?"

"My aunt's husband," was the reply. "They lived in Pocatello, Idaho. I think he has died. I want to turn their names in for temple work. They need to be endowed and sealed."

Richard Squire was found in the Social Security Death Index. He had died six months before his sister. The consultant got her answer with the help of the Lord, and her Uncle Richard had his ordinances completed. The thing that is truly amazing about this event is that there were at least four other workers at the reference counter whom the woman could have asked for help. Why did she ask that particular one? Just another coincidence?

In another instance, two young women from England were searching for the birth date of their great-grandfather and had not been able to find it in the indexes to Civil Registration for the year in which they believed he was born. They asked for help from a missionary working at the British Reference Desk. The missionary helped them look at some computer databases without success. Then he asked if they would mind if he searched the Civil Registration indexes again, and they said no. He pulled the microfiche index for the quarter in which they believed their great-grandfather was born, and there he was in the index. Astonished, the missionary suddenly noticed that the fiche was for another year and had been misfiled by someone else—right where they could find it. Just another coincidence?

In yet another instance, a brand-new missionary to the Library, just getting familiar with the available resources, asked a more experienced missionary for help using the International Genealogical Index® (IGI) on microfiche. The missionaries walked to a set of the IGI, but the one fiche they needed was missing. They walked over to another set, pulled the needed fiche, and as they placed it in the microfiche reader they began talking about the family they were searching for. A nonmember woman sitting at the next reader asked them if the family they were looking for was from Georgia. It was. The woman turned out to be related to the missionary, and the two of them happily exchanged family information. If the needed fiche had not been missing from the one set of the IGI, thus sending them to another set closer to the nonmember woman, the connection surely would not have been made!

Some may think that all of these instances, and many more just like them, are merely coincidences, but we think not. Anyone needing further inspiration or encouragement to begin or get back to their family history research need only read the many firsthand accounts of amazing occurrences that are told in the *LDS Church News* regular feature "Family History Moments." These miraculous "coincidences" enable research breakthroughs, unite distant family members, and allow temple work to be completed for those who are patiently waiting beyond the veil. The Spirit of Elijah guides and directs those who earnestly seek out their ancestors.

The employees and missionaries who work daily with patrons at the Family History Library and Family History Centers have observed that many of them are mature women. What is it that motivates women in particular to research their family history? One of the answers may be that women have a unique gift—the loving, mothering instinct. That instinct extends to family, both close and extended, and to friends and neighbors. That instinct motivates women to want to be of help to others, and that unique gift of love can extend to those beyond the veil.

If you are an older, mature women you may have opportunities to use your gifts in ways that are not always open to younger women. Some of the reasons for this may be:

• Your children are grown and moving from home, thus freeing you from some of the distractions that younger mothers face.

• You have retired from your job or career, or may be thinking of retiring.

• Lately you have had more free time for the things you always said you would do when you got around to it.

• You are feeling a bit at loose ends and need to be busy, but doing something of value. You need to feel you are still needed, still contributing.

• You have more of the time, ability, and assets needed for travel to cemeteries and record repositories.

• You have more patience!

Family history research is a perfect way for you to fill your needs and use your abilities.

A friend of ours in her late forties recently attended a family history conference with her husband and sister. The attendees were all subscribers to a newsletter for individuals researching one particular surname, and most were descendants of one common ancestor. Again, the majority were women, and our friend was one of the youngest there. One of the organizers even came up to greet her and said, "You are too young to be doing genealogy!" He was just joking, of course. Genealogical research is for individuals of all ages, but it does seem to appeal more to those who are past child-rearing or retired from full-time jobs in the workplace, and more especially to women. Our friend and her husband and sister were the only LDS people at the conference, and they had the opportunity to get to know some of their "cousins" and learn what motivates them in their genealogical work. One woman, active in a local genealogical organization in California, explained what family history research means to her:

> I was an only child. My mom was the youngest of two children, and her folks were both the babies of their families. My dad ran away from home when he was fifteen and never spoke about his family.
>
> When I got divorced years ago, I needed a time-consuming hobby. Searching out my roots became my hobby. My mom and I were never terribly close. The sharing of what we found in our research (she started before I did), and the brainstorming to try to find more, brought us closer, and certainly helped my admiration for my mom's mental capacities. This was long before we knew anything about taking classes. In the 1970s, Mom started taking classes at an LDS Family History Center. Whenever there was a seminar, I went too. I learned so much.
>
> One of the reasons I like to encourage people to find out what they can about their family is that I fear many of the younger generation today have a self-centered outlook on life. The teens seem to have no concept about the long-term repercussions of their actions today. They have no sense that they are unique and special. I feel that when they research about where they came from they develop a sense of the continuity of life, that many generations went into them being who they are, and they will jump into the chain and there will be generations down the road that will identify with them. I try to get them to look at their ancestors/parents as individuals with good and

bad, to realize that each person makes his or her own way, working with what God has given them. Each individual must be valued for what makes them special: one is a better reader, another a better track star, another a better artist; each is unique.

For me, part of the joy is in looking at old pictures of my dad's family and being able to see the "big ears" passed down, the missing eyeteeth, the second toe longer than the great toe, the blue eyes, and in knowing where the Irish gift of gab came from. Also, I have some sense of my dad as a person before I came into his life. For my mom, there is seeing the physical resemblance between all the females, checking out things such as substance abuse (alcohol or overeating), finding out where putting sugar on your pancakes came from, or where adding sugar, butter, salt, and pepper to stewed tomatoes you have plopped on buttered bread came from. As I learn more about the people I am from, I learn more about myself.

And there are weird things, like my dad's dad naming a daughter Bonnie [not the real name] in 1927, after my dad had lost contact with the family, and then my dad naming me Bonnie in 1939. We are the only Bonnies in the family, and our dads named both of us, and they were father and son, but had no contact with one another. Isn't that strange? Or is it God's hand in letting us know that we really do "belong in the same family" (though when we met we knew that right off the bat!).

Aside from myself, I love to do genealogy as I love to share in others' joy at surmounting a brick wall, at their sense of accomplishment as they find an answer that has eluded them for years. If I can be a part of helping them do that, it makes it better. I have many LDS friends (and even some family!), and when I can help them do what they consider a sacred duty, it makes me feel closer to them, closer to God, and of value to the world. And people don't mind coming to me, so I get to learn as I help them, too, which keeps my mind active.

Aren't her words marvelous? This woman has truly been touched by the Spirit of Elijah. She has been greatly blessed as she has blessed the lives of others, and you can be too. Family history research will benefit you in so many ways:

• It will give you a real sense of purpose.

• It will give you interesting challenges. Family history research is like detective work!

• It will be mentally stimulating, something that is needed in postretirement years.

• It will allow you to use and develop your thinking, analyzing, organizing, record-keeping, and writing skills.

• It will bring great joy into your life as you prepare names for temple work and then perform the ordinances for them.

Family history research will also allow you to do many great things:

• Develop a greater sense of continuity with generations past, present, and future.

• Develop a greater understanding of and appreciation for your ancestors and their lives, and the heritage they gave you.

• Positively contribute to that heritage.

• Teach your children and grandchildren more about their family and give them a greater sense of worth as a link in a great family chain of generations.

• Learn where some of your own aptitudes and personality and physical traits came from.

• Publish your family history as a lasting legacy to your research, work, and devotion to family.

• Uniquely express your love for your family.

As a member of the Church, you may have grown up hearing about the importance of doing family history research, and may have had an aunt who was known as the family genealogist. With all of that exposure over the years, if you didn't catch the spirit of family history work you might have caught the dread of it! However, modern technology, computers and the Internet, and simpler rules for submission of names for temple ordinances all contribute to making family history research a delight rather than a dread. In June 1999 the Church went on-line with its FamilySearch® website, so anyone who has access to the Internet can search the International Genealogical Index, Ancestral File™, and the Family History Library Catalog™. The site has SourceGuide™ (over 150 research outlines, an extensive glossary of word meanings, and Catalog Helper). The site provides the locations of Family History Centers worldwide. It has links to thousands of other genealogy-related websites, and offers collaboration lists. Family history researchers can even download Personal Ancestral File® 4.0 for use with Windows from the FamilySearch web page.

Family history research teaches us that there is still a lot in the world to learn. Older people sometimes think they are too old to learn new things or new ways to do things, but if you are involved in family history, you are learning and growing in spite of yourself. Classes are taught daily (Monday through Saturday) at the Family History Library and in many Family History Centers. Local genealogical societies teach classes for their members and the general public.

There are so many ways to get involved in family history research today. Here are just some of them:

- First of all, regularly attend the temple and do vicarious work for deceased individuals, especially your own family members when possible.

• Attend a family history research class at any one of a number of locations.

• Spend a few hours or days each month researching your own family history.

• Volunteer at the Family History Library or your local Family History Center. That is also a great way to learn.

• Volunteer to help with a stake extraction project.

• Assist a less-experienced fellow ward member with research.

• Become involved with your local genealogical society.

• Help organize a family reunion and prepare your own "Family History Moment" to share.

• Establish a family website on the Internet where family members can contribute to research and stay in touch with one another.

• Publish a family history.

• Write your own life story for your posterity.

In the November 21, 1998, *LDS Church News* "Family History Moment," Kirk P. Lovenbury said: "Information is out there on everyone's ancestors if they will only put forth the effort to find it. The key to family history [research] is patience, perseverance and prayer."

Family history work is not just another nice hobby. It is the Lord's work. If you will choose to undertake this work, and prayerfully ask him for his assistance, he and the Holy Spirit will guide and direct you, even place other helpers within your path, and you will gain your own "miraculous" experiences and witness of this divine work. It can even be your crowning glory. We pray that Heavenly Father's greatest blessings will be yours as you pursue your family history research!

# Notes

Barbara H. Baker was born in Kansas and raised in Colorado and Texas. She was converted to the Church in 1971 while a student at BYU, majoring in genealogical research. An accredited genealogist in English research, she has been employed at the Family History Library off and on since 1973 and continually since 1987. She is married and the mother of three sons.

Sandra S. Pitts received her degree in secondary education from the University of Utah. She taught art in Salt Lake City junior high schools for several years. She has held several positions in the Family History Department of the Church, and is accredited to do LDS and England research. She is presently a part-time consultant in the British Reference Unit. Sandra and her husband are the parents of three daughters and grandparents of two grandsons.

1. Gordon B. Hinckley, in Conference Report, April 1998, pp. 115–16.

*Chapter 9*

# Building an Intergenerational Family

### SANDRA MERRILL COVEY

*"To be held in remembrance from generation to generation"*
*(D&C 127:9)*

In the past, society has been a partner in sustaining us and helping us to create strong families. Family-friendly laws, media reinforcement, religious doctrine, and family values were the norm. But things have changed dramatically. More than ever, we need to take an active role in protecting and preserving the family. We need to build a strong support system that sustains and cements us together to fight the storms that are increasingly pounding the traditional family structure and trying to blow it off course.

As parents, aunts, uncles, brothers, sisters, cousins, and especially grandparents, we need to make becoming involved in family activities a priority. We need to have a family mission statement to guide and direct us. We need to be there for special occasions: birthdays, anniversaries, baby blessings, baptisms, mission farewells, graduations, recitals, programs, sports activities and games, school concerts, family reunions, and vacations.

We can become mentors to our grandchildren and family members. We can teach our grandchildren the skills we have mastered, such as how to sew, knit, or crochet; how to make cookies, pies, and candy; how to plant a garden or arrange flowers; how to repair cars and appliances; how to do woodwork; how to make stained-glass windows, bookcases, or patios. We can plan bird-watching trips, develop swimming skills, teach fishing or ice-skating. The challenge is to have the desire and the commitment. In this chapter I discuss the importance of developing a family mission statement, I propose the best ways to create intergenerational traditions, and I offer dozens of hands-on examples and stories with the hope that these suggestions will help you in your desire to build a strong extended and intergenerational family.

# Developing a Family Mission Statement

The Lord has a mission statement. It is: "To bring to pass the immortality and eternal life of man" (Moses 1:39). The Church has a mission statement: "To teach the gospel, perfect the Saints, and redeem the dead." These statements harmonize, integrate, guide, control, and give purpose. They are the frame of reference from which all decisions are made.

One way to strengthen our families is to develop and write a family mission statement—to identify, focus, discuss, and decide what is important to us and how to achieve it. Every family member should participate; even the youngest children can express their feelings. If the children are married you can write an intergenerational mission statement that provides guidance for the growing generations.

When writing a family mission statement, ask questions. What is our family about? How do we want to treat each other and speak to one another? What kind of atmosphere do we want in our home? What families inspire us and why do we admire them? What are our family goals and how might we accomplish them? What intergenerational traits or tendencies are we happy or unhappy with, and how do we make these changes? What are the principles we want to operate by? How do these principles tie into teaching our children the gospel, preparing them for missions, and leading them to Christlike lives? How can we contribute to society and become selfless and service-oriented yet develop the potential and talent of each person? What are the end and means, the vision and principles needed?

Writing a mission statement may take several weeks to complete. Write a draft, evaluate and discuss it, then make a final draft. You may print it up and give everyone a copy, keep it in your wallet or room, frame it, or make it into a plaque for your wall. One family I know had a plaque made of their mission statement and hung it outside their door. It said: "Inside this home are the sounds of love and the spirit of the gospel." It is important to see it, to study and review it, and to try to live by it. One of the Lord's purposes for man is to come unto Christ and be perfected in him. One of the essential purposes of the family is to create opportunities and experiences to develop a Christlike character and a gospel-centered family. Writing a mission statement can help you achieve this. Here are four examples of family mission statements. Notice the diversity between them:

1. "The mission of our family is to create a nurturing place of order, truth, love, happiness, and relaxation, and to provide opportunity for each person to become responsibly independent and effectively interdependent—in order to serve the threefold purpose of the Church through understanding and living the gospel of Jesus Christ."

2. "Our home will be a place where our family, friends, and guests find joy, comfort, peace, and happiness. We will seek to create a clean and orderly environment that is livable and comfortable. We will exercise wisdom in what we choose to eat, read, see, and do at home. We want to teach our children to love, to learn, to laugh—and to work and develop their own unique talent."

3. "And now I would that ye should be humble, and be submissive and gentle; easy to be entreated; full of patience and long-suffering; being temperate in all things; being diligent in keeping the commandments of God at all times; asking for whatsoever things ye stand in need, both spiritual and

temporal; always returning thanks unto God for whatsoever thing ye do receive. And see that ye have faith, hope, and charity, and then ye will always abound in good works" (Alma 7:23–24).

4. "No Empty Chairs." (In other words, we will always be there for each other, sustaining and supporting. No one will be left out.)

Make your mission statement brief or detailed, poetic or plain. It does not matter as long as it reflects what you want your family to be about and it inspires them to live up to that.

## Building Family Traditions

Family traditions include family rituals, celebrations, and meaningful events that you do in your family. They help you to understand who you are—that you are a part of a family that is a strong unit, that you love each other, that you respect and honor each other, that you celebrate one another's birthdays, holidays, and special events, and you build positive memories for everybody.

Through traditions, you reinforce the connection of the family. You give a feeling of belonging, of being supported, of being understood. You are committed to each other. You are a part of something that is greater than yourself. You express and show loyalty to each other. You need to be needed and you need to be wanted, and you're glad to be part of a family. When parents, grandparents, and children cultivate traditions that are meaningful to them, and then repeat these traditions, the family is strengthened.

Probably more than almost any other time, people love to celebrate their family traditions around important holidays.

They often come together from long distances. There's food. There's fun. There's laughter. There's sharing. And with many of these holidays, such as Easter, Thanksgiving, or Christmas, a unifying spiritual theme or purpose gives a renewing dimension to being together.

Many different traditions center around each holiday. Some standard traditions include Easter egg hunts, wearing green on St. Patrick's Day, trick-or-treating, Thanksgiving turkeys, Christmas caroling, and New Year's Day football games. Many traditions center around the kind of food that's served. Some traditions stem from particular countries or cultures, other traditions may have been passed down through the generations, and new traditions develop when people marry. All of these things give a sense of stability and of identity to the family.

All kinds of family traditions are tied in with long-repeated menus that if changed or varied, bring objections from family members. If I don't serve turkey and stuffing for Christmas, for example, it doesn't feel right.

My neighbors, Jan and Bob, have a tradition of inviting their extended family over on New Year's Day to visit and enjoy a wonderful meal of pork and sauerkraut. It is a German tradition that is supposed to bring you good luck and fortune throughout the entire year. They look forward to greeting each other and always leave the day open for this occasion.

When I married Stephen, I became acquainted with several new traditions. One tradition was around Valentine's Day. Every person in the family would always receive a Valentine in the mail with a one-dollar bill inside and these words: "Someone loves you—guess who?" They only stopped coming after Grandy, Stephen's mother, died. Other family members have since continued this tradition.

St. Patrick's Day is an important tradition in our family because Stephen and I lived in Ireland for three years. To celebrate St. Patrick's Day I would dress up in my green leprechaun outfit and appear uninvited in each of my children's classrooms. I would engage the whole class in singing Irish songs and would tell stories with an Irish lilt in my voice. Then I would give each child a shamrock cookie, and I'd pinch the boys and girls who weren't wearing green. The faces of my children would turn red on occasion, but they secretly loved it. This tradition has continued into the next generation, and now I visit my grandchildren in their classrooms. Through this tradition I hope to show them that I love them, that I want to be a part of their lives, and that they are an important part of my life.

On Memorial Day we remember those loved ones who have passed away. My own mother was from Berlin, Germany. To honor her on this holiday, I will serve a typical German meal of rouladen, purple cooked cabbage, potato pancakes, and applesauce. Our family will recall how she, her sisters, and mother all joined The Church of Jesus Christ of Latter-day Saints and came to America from Germany. We reminisce about her life, recall tender experiences, and teach the grandchildren about their heritage.

Families can establish decorating traditions for the holidays and special occasions. Decorating is one of my favorite pastimes, so I go all out for my family on every occasion I can. I try to have a lovely centerpiece on our kitchen table to celebrate birthdays or holidays. There's nothing like large wood rabbits, leprechauns, witches, ghosts, Valentine's hearts,

Happy New Year's banners, gingerbread men, or tall wooden soldiers to brighten up our front porch during the holidays. I have collected flags from all over that display what holiday or season it is, so my kids will immediately know what occasion we are celebrating. My daughter Jenny teases me that the minute I take down decorations from one holiday I start putting up decorations for the next event, but I enjoy this! And I love watching my children and grandchildren notice and delight in the decorations.

The point is that holidays provide an ideal time to build traditions. They happen every year. It's easy to create a sense of anticipation and fun as well as meaning and camaraderie around them. As parents, we have developed and nurtured these family traditions. As grandparents, we want to encourage them to continue. This takes time, effort, and commitment. But if we don't do it, who will?

## Sew What's Club

You don't have to be limited to establishing traditions around scheduled holidays. Start traditions for tradition sake at any time of the year. Find a need and meet it.

When I first married into my husband's large family of uncles, aunts, cousins, and grandparents, I was concerned that I would never be able to get to know them all, or be able to put a name to a face. I was pleasantly surprised when I was invited to join the women of the family for their monthly luncheon of the "Sew What's" club. Everyone was to bring a potluck food item and her hand sewing or mending (yes, we did mend socks in those days). It was a delightful time, and over the months I did get to know and enjoy all the ladies as they told about funny situations, stories, and family tales. I not only got to know and love the current generation but also felt a bond and appreciation for those who had passed on.

## The Dearies

My husband's mother, Grandy, was a loving, vivacious woman. She always called everyone "dearie," a term of endearment. Her home was the gathering place for holiday get-togethers. After she died, the cousins were afraid they would lose touch with each other because Grandy was gone. They would not have a central meeting place. To prevent this from happening, the granddaughters from each family started a quarterly dinner party with their husbands, calling it "The Dearies," in memory of Grandy. Each family takes a turn hosting the party. They discuss genealogy projects, enjoy a meal, reminisce about past times, and renew and strengthen their friendships.

## Nursery Rhymes and Songs for Generations

When our children were young, I used to rock them to sleep by singing nursery rhymes and songs. All of the children learned them by heart. We sang them everywhere—at home, at the park, and driving in the car. Each of the nine children had a favorite they loved: "Polly Put the Kettle On," "Hot Cross Buns," "A Tisket, a Tasket," "Bobby Shafto's Gone to Sea," and the "Paw Paw Patch," to name a few.

Now, in our grandchildren's playroom, we have painted the nursery rhyme pictures and song titles on the walls, with a notation: "Colleen's favorite, 'Oh Dear, What Can the Matter Be,' " "Joshua's song, 'Do You Know the Muffin Man,' " or " 'Cock A Doodle Doo,' Catherine's rhyme." We also put the family's favorite poems, songs, stories, and sayings on the walls in full color illustrations. Some of these include "Peter Rabbit," "The Three Billy Goats Gruff," "The Elephant's Child," "The Wolf and the Seven Little Kids," "Hush Little Baby," "I Am a Child of God," "Twinkle, Twinkle Little Star," "Rain, Rain Go Away," "Lady Bug Fly Away Home," and "Starlight, Starbright." On the ceiling of this grandchildren's room is Mother Goose, of course, flying on her broom through a cloudy, star-filled sky. To the delight of my grandchildren, the stars even glow in the dark when the lights are off.

The fun part is that all our children have read and sung the very same nursery rhymes and songs to their children, and so they all know and love the same tunes, rhymes, and melodies. Those best-loved verses will continue to be passed down from generation to generation with the same fervor and excitement as they were originally taught. Reading and singing is a great family tradition, but the best part is that, like Mother Goose herself, I know that my "melodies will never die, while nurses sing or babies cry."

## Simple Ways to Keep in Touch

Sometimes the simplest gestures are the grandest gestures. Children respond to gifts of love and do not care what the gift costs or where it comes from.

I have only a few memories of my maternal grandmother, Grandmother Bienert, because she died at an early age. I vividly remember the smell of brown sugar saturating her kitchen pantry. She used to come on the bus to visit our home once a week. She always brought me a chocolate Hershey bar, which I remember being the grandest gift. Unfortunately, for me, she also made sure I had a supply of cod-liver oil to be taken daily.

My own mother used to visit our children, and they waited in awe and anticipation for her ritual of opening her purse and producing a pack of gum for each child to have for their own. A bag of gold would not have brought more happiness.

Sending a simple postcard addressed to your grand-daughter makes her feel important. A personal letter just to her, a phone call, a fax, or an E-mail lets her know she is remembered. A private date with a grandson to get a malt or a breakfast at McDonald's can be fun and rewarding. You speak volumes to a granddaughter by framing and hanging in a prominent place in your home, where she and others will see it, a picture she painted. These small gestures will be remembered and valued.

I know one grandmother who has a phobia about leaving her home for fear of catching a disease. She rarely goes any-where or has visitors, yet she loves her grandchildren and wants to be a part of their lives. Each night at eight she tele-phones her ten-year-old grandson and they read the Book of Mormon together. It is their special time and they have grown close because of their simple ritual.

## Family Letters and Newsletters

When loved ones are living away from home because of a mission, study abroad, business relocation, college, or even a permanent move, their letters become a vital link in keeping family members in touch with each other. In addition to writing letters to family members living away, you can start a family newsletter.

At one point in our lives, our children, married and non-married, were spread throughout the country and on foreign missions. Our daughter, Catherine, living in Michigan at the time, suggested a family newsletter and volunteered to be the editor. Each party was asked to send her pictures and news updates by a certain date. If they weren't in on time, we knew it, because she would call, and the "wrath of Cath" compelled you to submit it immediately. We received the newsletter every three months and devoured each edition. Filled with cleverly written episodes of family life, family recipes, inside family jokes, and well-earned life experiences, this newsletter was anxiously awaited and was well worth the effort.

# The Information Age

During my childhood it was a special occasion when an aunt and uncle, or another relative, would come to visit. Most came from long distances and had to drive for hours or even days to get there.

Today it is easier and cheaper to keep in touch with loved ones. With families spread out not only throughout the country but the world as well, the information age is at our fingertips. You can personally speak to those children, grandchildren, and family members scattered around the world for reasonable costs. There is nothing more satisfying than hearing the voice of a loved one. A call on a birthday, graduation, anniversary, or special occasion shows your love and concern and connects you once again. Make those who live far away feel missed and included in the family interactions and dialogue.

In addition to phone calls, the majority of families have a home computer, if not one at the office. We can communicate quickly and daily using E-mail or sending faxes. Many families even set up their own websites. If you do not know how to do this, one of your children or grandchildren will.

## Inexpensive Family Activities

Getting together as a family does not have to take money or extravagance; we need only use our imaginations to bring our families together for simple bonding activities. Since everyone's life is busy, as I mentioned before, build family get-togethers around events that are already scheduled into people's calendars, such as holidays, anniversaries, birthdays, programs, sports, concerts, and other events and activities that you would naturally celebrate.

A divorced mother with little money but much love and creativity could not afford to take her grandchildren on trips or out to dinner, so she created her own special occasions. She would often pitch a tent in her backyard, invite everyone to bring their own flashlights and sleeping bags, and spread out on the lawn, tent, and trampoline. They would make plenty of popcorn, caramel candy, and snacks, tell ghost stories, sing songs, and watch old movies on a makeshift screen made from a sheet.

If your families live in close proximity, you can enjoy gathering together after sporting events such as basketball and football games. I love the football season. Living in Provo, Utah, a university town, we are consumed with BYU football.

All of our family who live nearby come to the games. Our married children, grandchildren, brothers and sisters and their families, cousins, aunts and uncles, and their friends all come. After the game, everyone drops by for my special hot stew, garlic bread, and chocolate cake. Family members interact, enjoy one another, and mingle in a relaxed atmosphere. We never know who or how many will show up—but we know it will be fun, exciting, and spirited.

Often families plan a yearly activity at a local amusement park. Children anxiously anticipate it and the grandparents should not miss out. There are covered, shady picnic grounds and plenty of benches surrounding the amusement rides. Grandparents can help the little ones in the kid-sized amusement park, leaving the parents free to supervise and join the older children in their pursuits.

An outdoor barbecue in the backyard, at the beach, or up the canyon is delightful. Dutch oven cooking is a tradition many families enjoy. Often a neighborhood or local park can be used for summer family gatherings. Adults play games like volleyball, horseshoes, and badminton, and children color on the sidewalks with chalk, play hopscotch, or jump the rope. You could even set up a square dance or a game of flag football.

Take the grandkids to the driving range and hit a bucket of balls. Take them to rock-climbing walls, paint-ball shoot-outs, and water parks. Go tubing down a river, fishing in a nearby stream, or rowing on a lake. My husband takes the grandkids on Honda rides on his ATC. They love it.

In the winter go ice-skating, sledding, or snowmobiling. Nothing's more invigorating than a good snowball fight or building a snowman. The possibilities are endless. Be creative and make the effort.

## Family Firesides and Temple Excursions

My friend Margaret is a first-rate scholar and scripturalist. Even as a young mother raising a large family, she set aside two hours each day to study the scriptures. She told me that one of her incentives came from the tradition of meeting once a month for a family fireside, where lively religious discussions were enjoyed. You had to be eighteen years old to attend. A religious topic was assigned and each family member came doctrinally prepared to discuss it.

Many families I know have similar meetings monthly or quarterly. Sometimes only the married couples are invited. One intergenerational family I know invites all the young adult cousins to meet together regularly and choose the Book of Mormon or other major scriptures or religious book for study that year. Each family takes turns conducting the meeting and leading the discussion.

Often families will invite all those who are endowed to meet together for a temple session and gather for dinner afterwards at one of their homes. These interactions take foresight and planning, but help build gospel study and fellowship.

## Baby Blessings and Baptisms

Whenever a new baby is blessed or a child is baptized it is a wonderful time for family members to gather together in their honor. A baby book can be signed by brothers and sisters, aunts and uncles, and cousins, with comments and advice to the new baby and mother. For example, "A sure cure remedy for colic," "How to get by on three hours sleep a night," or "Advice for nursing mothers."

You can plan a small program, with talks and musical numbers by family members. Have a potluck dinner. Present a set of scriptures to the newly baptized child. Often, parents put together a video or have a picture display. Gifts are presented. Photos are taken. These are milestones in the lives of our loved ones and it is appropriate we honor them.

## Family Picture Gallery

My mother-in-law had a wonderful Rogues' Gallery in her bedroom. The family seemed to congregate there and loved looking at their family pictures. As a new bride, this gallery helped me learn who all the relatives were.

I borrowed this idea from her and for years have covered the walls in our family room from floor to ceiling with pictures of our family at all stages of their lives. These include pictures of our fathers, mothers, grandparents, and great-grandparents; our black and white wedding pictures; Stephen—when he had hair; me—pencil thin; baby and school pictures of our nine children taken through the years; pictures of them with no teeth, with freckles, zits, and braces, high school proms, sports and cheerleading pictures, graduations, college, mission, and wedding pictures. We have many family group shots, and now I also have a grandchildren's wall.

Whenever I think of my children I don't necessarily think of how they look and act today. I'm flooded with memories of familiar expressions they used, favorite outfits they wore. Baby, toddler, preschool, teen, young adult—all these images flash before my mind as I see the finished product before me. I remember the ages and stages, the looks, laughter, tears, failures, and the triumphs.

A glance at this picture wall is like having your whole life flash before you in a few seconds. I'm flooded with memories, nostalgia, pride, joy, and renewal. We have lots of scrapbooks, and I enjoy those, too. But this is our family—our life—all around me. And I love it.

Everyone who comes to our house is immediately drawn to the picture gallery. They notice the family resemblances of an aunt, cousin, or grandparent, or how a particular grandchild looks exactly like their mother or father did at the same age. This is our family, our heritage. The picture gallery reminds them they belong, they are loved, they are linked with the past and the future. One of the main functions of family life is to build positive memories that tie the children to an eternal family, to teach them the gospel, and to teach them how to love and serve each other and the Lord, so they will have a solid foundation.

## Ten-Generation Charts

A few years ago, our son-in-law, Matthew, gave us a most unusual and wonderful Christmas gift. He bought two copies of the circular ten-generation charts and, studying our files and research, wrote in beautiful penmanship the names of all our ancestors. He framed them beautifully. He made one chart for my husband's parents' lines and another chart for my parents' lines. In doing the research Matt found about fifty names that did not have some temple work performed, and so our family was able to complete the work for those ancestors.

We hung these circular charts in our genealogy room, along with pictures, books, and genealogical information. One can see at a glance the remaining research and work on different lines that needs to be completed. Our children and grandchildren often look at these charts with great interest and questions about their heritage.

## *Family Ancestor Portraits*

Another son-in-law, Dave, found portraits of my husband's great-great-grandfather, Willard Richards, and my great-great-grandfather, Marriner Wood Merrill, in the Church museum. He had duplicate copies made and had them beautifully framed. Under each portrait he had an inserted quote, which in itself told of the stature and character of the man.

Willard Richards was a doctor, the founder of the *Deseret News*, an Apostle, and a beloved friend to the Prophet Joseph Smith. His insert reads: "Brother Joseph, you did not ask me to cross the river with you . . . you did not ask me to come to Carthage—you did not ask me to come to jail with you—and do you think I would forsake you now? But I will tell you what I will do; if you are condemned to be hung for 'treason,' I will be hung in your stead, and you shall go free. 'You cannot,' the Prophet said. 'I will,' Elder Richards replied."[1]

Marriner Wood Merrill's insert is similarly moving. I want my children and grandchildren to feel a sense of gratitude, loyalty, pride, and responsibility when they reflect on these men, their ancestors. With these portraits hanging prominently on our library wall, my children and grandchildren will gain an interest in knowing them.

## Family Ancestor Stories

President Spencer W. Kimball wisely advised the members of the Church: "We ought to encourage our children to know their relatives. We need to talk of them, make effort to correspond with them, visit them, join family organizations, etc."[2] Parents and grandparents have the responsibility and privilege to help their children and other posterity learn about and know their ancestors. This means learning about who they were, how they lived their lives, what sacrifices they made, what struggles they dealt with, and how they made a difference.

Family records, genealogy research, journals, and life stories are good resources, but nothing is more powerful or compelling than a family story, told and repeated over and over until it becomes a part of your family oral history. The characters can become so real and so much a part of the family dialogue that children feel they know them personally.

One favorite story our family tells is about Great-grandmother Merrill, who wanted to have her ears pierced. Her husband was adamant that she should not, as he didn't think it was natural. He would say to her, "If the good Lord wanted you to have holes in your ears, he would have made them that way." At the time, she was expecting a child. When the baby girl was born, she had a tiny hole in each ear, just as if they had each been pierced. Great-grandfather was miffed. Needless to say, Great-grandmother had her ears pierced.

Stephen's mother, Grandy—a woman who never missed a birthday, a performance, or a graduation of anyone, and who thrived on bringing over 176 living relatives together for special occasions—gave each child and grandchild a set of scriptures when the new quad came out. In each copy she inscribed her testimony in the front pages. It read:

> All my ancestors, my father, my mother, grandparents, and great grandparents on both sides of my family believed and testified to the divinity of the Savior, the truthfulness of Joseph Smith's vision that God does live and Jesus is the Christ—that the LDS Church is the kingdom of God on the earth and of a living prophet. Each of you is so precious to me. I love you dearly and pray these scriptures will inspire, lift, and teach you the truths so we can be together as a family, not only for time, but for all eternity.

Grandy loved and honored her ancestors because she knew them. She read their journals and letters and told us stories of their courage and valiance.

Perhaps your heritage does not have generations of faithful Saints. Maybe your own parents or even you are the beginning of the spiritual foundation of faith for your family. That was the case with my own mother. Born and raised in Berlin, Germany, she almost starved to death as a child during the first World War. Her wish for Christmas was to have a loaf of bread to eat all by herself. In those days a banana was such a luxury that until the day she died she couldn't eat one without her eyes filling up with tears.

The sister missionaries came and taught her mother and two sisters Lilly and Katie. She and her father resisted. When the missionary discussions were taught, she use to fluff up the couch cushions and fuss around the room, making as much noise as politely possible. Then she and her father would leave hand in hand, vowing they would never join. But in the end, she couldn't resist. She knew the Church was true and had to act on it. She and her mother and two sisters were to be baptized and go to America. Her father was devastated, "Oh, Erika, not you, not my little one. Will you go and leave me also?" Erika answered, "I must, Father, for it's true."

As I grow older, I realize that everything we have and enjoy and take for granted was bought with a price. Sickness, suffering, courage, and even death made this valley safe for us—our homes, our lovely ward chapel, the temple, the BYU, our testimonies. Even our righteousness is bought with a price because of the beliefs and sacrifices of those who came before. We are harvesting what they planted, and our posterity must know this.

## Renewal at Family Retreats and Vacations

Families that have a cabin, homestead, or traditional vacation spot find it meaningful to return to the same place year after year. This brings a sense of stability and connection. Our daughter Colleen says: "You can count on it being the same, year after year. It's as if nothing changes, and you want it to stay that way."

We have some old family cabins on Hebgen Lake in Montana, just outside of West Yellowstone. Grandfather Richards started going there some seventy-five years ago. At Hebgen we become acquainted with and renew friendships with aunts, uncles, distant cousins, and relatives we may only see occasionally. We catch frogs under the dock, build sand castles on the shores of the lake, swim in the freezing waters, catch rainbow trout, spot moose drinking from the shores of the meadow, play volleyball on the beach, ride our motor-cycles to Prayer Rock, water-ski, read, and visit for hours on end. No one would miss it for anything. At Hebgen we renew and strengthen the bond between parent and child, brother and sister, grandparent and grandchild. Up until ten years ago, we had no telephone or television there.

One of the fun traditions Stephen and I started at Hebgen Lake is the Pirate Treasure Hunt. We sneak into West Yellowstone and raid the dollar store, buying all kinds of inexpensive items to fill our pirate's chest: balls, Slinkies, magic ink, bear bells, Indian canoes, plastic handcuffs, rabbit foot chains, rubber knives, bow-and-arrow sets, coin purses, yo-yos, slingshots, and Indian bead jewelry. We load the chest, and pile into the boat—along with shovels, a pirate flag, and handwritten clues burned at the edges to look old and authentic.

After beaching the boat on Goat Island, we search for a place on the beach to bury the treasure. We cover the hiding place with clean sand and throw brush on it so that it looks untouched. Finally, we run all over the island leaving clues in trees and shrubs and under rocks. Then we scatter coins—pennies, nickels, dimes, and even silver dollars—for the little kids to find.

Half dead, we return to the mobs of kids at the beach and wave an old battered pirate flag with its black skull and bones. We scream that we scared off some pirates who left their buried treasure behind.

Everyone—kids, grown-ups, and even our dog—piles into boats, dinghies, and Ski-Doos to invade the island. They scramble and run from clue to clue until they discover the treasure. The loot is distributed, and the tradition is complete.

It is wonderful to feel a sense of stability and connection by returning to the same place, year after year, and it doesn't matter where you go as a family as long as you are able to spend quality time together and create stronger family ties. You might enjoy renting a houseboat on Lake Powell, watching plays at the annual Shakespeare Festival, visiting temples around the country, attending education week at a college campus, backpacking in the Tetons, visiting your favorite national park, or going on a fishing trip.

Families anticipate and carefully plan their time together so they can reconnect as a family and continue building valuable relationships, visiting and conversing together in a relaxed atmosphere.

Part of the joy that comes from family vacations is the planning process itself. To talk about, anticipate, prepare, reflect on past vacations, and look forward to the upcoming vacation can be as fulfilling as the vacation itself.

## Essay Party

The Hickman family had an intergenerational family party to honor their grandmother who had died a few years ago. Everyone was assigned to write an essay about her, telling some personal experiences or observations about her life.

After a delicious dinner, everyone gathered around to share their essays by reading them aloud to the group. As the evening wore on, the stories became more funny, and similar themes were often repeated. Grandmother drove a bright red car with a stick shift and, according to legend, was a wild and crazy driver. Relatives were holding their sides from laughing and soon one story led to another. The grandma had a painting of a partially clad woman hanging in her bathroom. Almost everyone mentioned it, and one cousin declared, "I always thought it was a relative." Those who attended the party were well rewarded by the warmheartedness and family bonding. They laughed and cried together as they relived choice memories. They also printed up a bound booklet of all these essays for those unable to attend.

## Handmade Items to Treasure

Rebecca, my daughter-in-law, has a beautifully framed picture box on her entry wall, which contains a hand-cut crystal bowl, elegantly designed. It belonged to her great-great-grandmother, who painstakingly carried it with her while crossing the plains. When seeing this treasure, people ask immediate questions about this remarkable pioneer woman. It gives Rebecca the opportunity to share the story and heritage with her family and other loved ones.

My own mother loved to knit. Whenever any family member had a new baby, my mother would knit a pink, blue, and yellow blanket for the infant. She also made a unique wardrobe of tiny newborn baby booties of every color and would place these in a long, narrow box and present them to the new mother. It is a trademark in the family. Every mother treasures her box of knitted baby booties as a keepsake and remembrance of their newborn and of my mother.

At Christmas, my mother would give each family member a new pair of knitted houseslippers in wild, bright colors. The old ones from last year were nearly worn out and we could hardly wait for their replacement. On special occasions—birthdays, weddings, anniversaries—mother knitted a cozy comforter or afghan in the colors of your choice. These hand-knit items are treasured and adored as recipients remember the sustaining love of my mother, their sister, aunt, cousin, or grandmother.

## The Family Quilt

One grandmother I know has always enjoyed the art of quilting. She designs new or makes traditional patterns that she skillfully creates on her quilting frames set up in her family room. As the family has grown and expanded, she supervises the completion of a family quilt to be given to newly called missionaries or newlywed brides. Each individual family is given material and is to design a large square that tells about their heritage, such as joining the Church in England, traveling across the plains, building the temple in St. George, serving a mission in Germany, and so forth.

All of the squares are given to the grandmother who assembles them and provides the backing and design. She hosts a quilting party where the quilt is assembled and presented to the honored guest. Each family explains what their quilt square represents, telling stories of their family history and why it is meaningful to them. The new missionary or bride has a renewed sense of family heritage and the quilt becomes a valued heirloom to be handed down to future generations.

# It's Never Too Late to Begin Again

On one occasion I accompanied my husband to Florida, where he spoke to a group of extremely wealthy retired couples about the importance of the three-generation family. Their lives seemed to center around playing golf, meeting friends for dinner, playing bridge, and country club socials. Family involvement was not a major force or priority to them. They would see their children and grandchildren at Easter, Christmas, and occasionally for a short family vacation. They justified these actions by saying it gave their children more independence from them and that they didn't want their families to be too socially, financially, or emotionally dependent on them. After much discussion, many opened up and admitted they felt guilty for not being more involved or willing to give more input and family support.

Often you see families that indeed are too immersed in each other, but these retired people were too detached, too independent, and they knew it. They wanted to achieve a healthy balance and were anxious to discuss ways to achieve it. They wanted to begin again.

Grandparents, aunts, uncles, brothers, and sisters can always be involved with the family. There is often a need for providing ongoing support and affirmation, for being there for others, for giving a sense of vision of what the intergenerational or extended family is all about. You never "retire" from the family.

A business acquaintance of my husband confessed that in his quest to climb the ladder of success, he felt that he had missed his children's childhoods. His mind and heart were focused on other things and he did not give family relationships his top priority. It was only now, in his late fifties, that he realized the importance of being a loving husband, father, and grandfather, and he desperately wanted to reclaim his children. He found true wealth not in money, prestige, or position, but in genuine familial relationships.

He was very excited about building a three-generation home on the beach—a place where children and grandchildren could come and have precious times with their cousins, aunts, uncles, and other relatives. He showed his understanding of what it takes to build an intergenerational family when he said: "It is a common project we are all working on together. In a sense I am reaching my children through involvement with their children, and they love it. I have a chance to redeem myself and do it right this time around."

It is never too late to begin again. It is never too late to show interest in a child or grandchild. And it is never too late to create a family mission statement. One sure way to live forever is to build and develop a meaningful relationship with your children and grandchildren, for they will remember you and they will tell their children stories about you just as you have about your parents and grandparents. The spirit of Elijah lives and is contagious: "He shall turn the heart of the fathers to the children, and the heart of the children to their fathers" (Malachi 4:6). You will never regret making the effort to build and develop an intergenerational family. In fact, this effort will reward you and bring you more joy than you can possibly imagine.

## Notes

Sandra Merrill Covey and her husband, Stephen R. Covey, are the parents of nine children and grandparents of thirty-three. Sister Covey is a graduate of Brigham Young University and a frequent speaker for Education Week and other conferences and seminars. She has served as a ward and stake Young Women's president and a stake Relief Society president, and she accompanied her husband when he was called as a mission president to Ireland. A soprano soloist, she has served on the Utah Opera Board, the Provo Arts Council, and the Utah Valley Symphony Board.

1. See B. H. Roberts, *A Comprehensive History of The Church of Jesus Christ of Latter-day Saints,* 6 vols. (Provo, Utah: Brigham Young University Press, 1965), 2:283.
2. Spencer W. Kimball, in Conference Report, October 1974, p. 161.

# Chapter 10

*Chapter 10*

# Called to Preach

**LILLIAN S. ALLDREDGE**

*"And more blessed are you because you are called of me to preach my gospel" D&C 34:5*

We were both over fifty years old when my husband and I received our call to preside over a Church mission. I recall how my heart was then filled with many tender emotions. I was grateful for the opportunity to serve in this important work of the Lord. I knew that many of our leaders referred to missionary work as "the life blood of the Church." Deep in my heart I had always wanted to go on a mission, and I knew that my husband had dreamed of returning to missionary service since the day he returned from his first mission as a young man.

But with those feelings of joy came also the reality of leaving our children, grandchildren, parents, brothers, sisters, and friends, as well as leaving the security and comforts of the life that had become so important to us. I knew it would be difficult to leave dear ones for three years; I also knew any sacrifice my husband and I might make would pale in comparison with the greatest sacrifice already made by our Savior, and I knew that our own sacrifices would be abundantly countered by the blessings we would continually receive at his hand while serving.

It was more than two months after our call before we knew we were to serve in the England London Mission. I thought, England, London! How wonderful! President Gordon B. Hinckley, whom both of us dearly love, had served part of his first mission there. In reading his description of London, I learned that he had been captivated by every part of this "jewel of the far flung British empire." The then young missionary viewed the scene from the third-floor window of the European Mission office at 5 Gordon Square, as it then appeared: "black taxicabs weaving in and out of traffic, little horns mounted on the outside. Bobbies with nightsticks walked the streets. Red mailboxes on street corners symbolized a postal system whose efficiency was unrivaled anywhere in the world. London was intoxicating. The pace, the cosmopolitan nature of the population, the sophisticated culture—it was invigorating for a young man from Salt Lake City. He came to believe that no one could 'live in London for long without developing a love for the place.' "[1] As I read, I realized London would also prove invigorating for this not-so-young lady missionary.

I began to study all I could about the country in terms of Church history. I learned that "British contributions to the Church have taken two main forms: providing a training ground for many early Church leaders, and helping to build and sustain the fledgling Church through the influx of British immigrants. . . . All of the men who have served as President of the Church, from Joseph Smith to Ezra Taft Benson, trace their ancestry back to the British Isles. . . . All of the Church Presidents except Joseph Smith, Harold B. Lee, and Spencer W. Kimball labored as missionaries in Great Britain."[2] These men of God had conducted the Church into the twentieth century; now it would be our privilege and blessing to be there as we entered the twenty-first century. I knew that the Lord would prepare missionaries for this pivotal time who would serve under us and be able to make major contributions to the Church in England.

Initially, I felt that serving a mission would be a life-changing experience. At the end of our mission it had proved to be just that for both my husband and me. In fact, I took note of how many others—the young or the mature, men and women, serving in like manner—found the experience life-altering. Although each of us came as servants to London through individual inspiration, each of our lives were uniquely changed in great measure to the benefit of every individual.

There was another reason why I was so thrilled to be assigned to go to the England London Mission. I prized the assignment because my ancestors were born and lived there. One of those English ancestors raised his family there, except during the period when he was in Germany translating the

Bible into an authorized version. This early missionary became a martyr for the truth when he was burned at the stake at Smithfield, just outside London, in 1555. That ancestor, John Rogers, was a man of faith who gave his all so that I and others of God's children might know the truths of the gospel. I read again of some of his earlier work as found in the Bible Dictionary: "In 1537 Thomas Matthew (whose real name was John Rogers) issued, also with the king's license, an edition that followed Tindale's as regards the N.T. [New Testament] and half the O.T. [Old Testament], the remainder being taken from Coverdale's."[3]

The soon-to-be martyred John Rogers made only one request of the officials who pronounced his death sentence. Having been long imprisoned, he wanted to see his wife and ten children just once before his death. Coldly refused, he was told, "You have no wife nor children." My noble ancestor was burned at the stake, as were others, because he was involved, with the previous monarch's approval, in translating the Bible into English. It was now my privilege to preach gospel truths in England and try with all my heart, might, and strength to serve faithfully as he had done. My knowledge of him gave me increased dedication to serve my mission as courageously and faithfully as I could.

During my many moments of reflection before and after we arrived in London, I was filled with a great desire to help every missionary sent to the England London Mission to consider ways they might make their time in that historic mission of greatest worth. I knew my husband was already well prepared intellectually and spiritually to help each one find great compensations for service in the mission field.

# Closeness Comes When Missionaries Unite in Purpose

During one of those reflective times in London, while sitting in our new-home-away-from-home, our mission home, I began recalling the treasured moments our senior missionaries had shared with me as they told of ministering to others as well as finding ways to meet their individual needs and responsibilities.

Accepting a mission call, they found a complete commitment to the Lord; taking all of one's time and energy. Concentrated effort in a *more blessed* work as this brought with it abundant benefits. Over and over again the senior missionary couples expressed the joy they experienced as they felt close to the Holy Spirit. One couple explained that the closeness they felt to each other was strengthened because both of them focused on the same things. This differed from most of their married life, when the husband's thoughts and concerns were centered on earning a living while the wife's thoughts were centered on the activities of their family and home. But now, for the first time in many years, their first thoughts in the morning and their last thoughts at night were on the same work, the same people, the same challenges, and the same situations. And when the focus was on proclaiming the word of the Lord, they entered into a united companionship that included the Holy Ghost. One of those sister missionaries reported: "We have such closeness as a couple, but in reality it is a threesome because we are working for peace and trying to bring the hearts of God's children to Him. Try to imagine how wonderful that feeling is! I feel it daily here on our mission.

I love to teach the truths of the gospel, watch it change lives, and strengthen my own testimony."

For me, it was a recurring practice to see dedicated senior couples come into the mission field to serve the Lord. They were couples of great commitment. They would do anything we asked, even though many of the assignments called for work that was not particularly fun or easy. The duty didn't matter. Those couple missionaries found a way to do the task well, and in so performing they blessed people's lives wherever they went. I feel confident that the same is true in any mission.

After a particularly difficult assignment, one elder was speaking in a zone conference. His missionary wife leaned over to me and said, "I am so proud of him." I realized how good it was for them to be there together and share their mission experience. Virtues in their lives that had been taken for granted before were now more obvious—and obviously more appreciated. They not only shared a full and rewarding experience together, but also their attitude of dedicated service taught all who observed them.

## Family Receives Added Blessings

I know how difficult it was for us to leave our home, our children, and our grandchildren. At first it seemed that the concerns and responsibilities left behind would be a burden. But as our service became focused on the things the Lord would have us do, the burden of worrying about those left behind was lifted.

One couple, in order to serve their mission, left behind a beautiful home and five older children and several grandchildren. While on their mission, they lived in a small but expensive flat, and at night they would move their small table and chairs and pull their bed out from the wall in their one-room apartment. At the time one of their daughters was in the process of divorcing, and they were concerned for her welfare. The husband's mother had also suffered a stroke. When they reflected on events at home that occurred during their mission, they said, "If we had been home, we would have worried uncontrollably, but being away we put our trust in the Lord and things were taken care of. Our mother did survive. Our other children reached out to our daughter when she needed them. We saw miracles happen as we were taken away from the monetary efforts that had kept us so busy at home. Our attitude became more positive, and we loved the way we saw the hand of the Lord bless our lives and the lives of our family members."

Another sister missionary reflected on the insights gained through their service as a couple missionary in England. She recorded: "Our experience of first serving a mission in Nauvoo gave us spiritual insights that we hadn't quite expected. To learn of those early Saints, their hard work, their dedication, their sacrifices, their spiritual vision was, indeed, humbling for us. We left there with a feeling that we had more to contribute, and that our service paled in comparison to that of those early Saints. Our call to serve in the England London Mission gave us an opportunity to further contribute. As we saw the struggle of our Saints in small English branches, we realized that they, too, are pioneers of a different era, an era that requires the same hard work, dedication, sacrifice, and spiritual vision of their forebears who left that isle to bolster the kingdom in America. Our service there was testimony building for us as we strived to incorporate those same qualities into our own lives."

Another missionary couple experienced a true miracle in their lives. While serving their mission, their daughter, who had been married for ten years and had been unable to conceive, wrote with delight to say she and her husband were expecting a baby. In time they were blessed with a little girl. Her parents felt this blessing was a direct result of their prayers. And their daughter felt it was a blessing that came because of her parents' missionary service. When it was time to come home, the daughter wrote somewhat humorously, "You can't leave your mission. We need more children."

"I learned early on," reported an elderly sister missionary, "that blessings continually flow into my life from our Heavenly Father. So when I was called at seventy-five years of age to go on a proselyting mission to the London England Mission, I knew it was a blessing from God. I was happily surprised to learn that my first companion, who was from Spain, had been converted by one of my former early-morning seminary students. I had preached the gospel in a classroom years before and saw years later the rewards of it in the mission field."

A sister missionary told of a wonderful present she and her missionary husband received. They met a very receptive young man who, when they taught him, said, "I've been waiting for you!" He was baptized that January, about the same time their thirty-year-old granddaughter returned to Church activity.

The lives of these missionaries are a fulfillment of a statement by President Thomas S. Monson: "I commend the many couples who now go forth to serve. Leaving the comforts of home, the companionship of family, they walk hand in hand as eternal companions, but also hand in hand with God as His representatives to a faith-starved world."[4]

## The Mission Receives Great Blessings

The branches, wards, and stakes of our mission literally shone with the gold dust that the senior missionaries seemed to sprinkle everywhere they went. We could feel their influence and see the difference they were making.

I think of a situation in particular. One little ward was struggling and had nearly collapsed as a unit. They had a wonderful bishop, but the ward was full of first-generation members who had trouble with the basics of the gospel. A senior missionary couple was assigned to the ward and began helping the bishop. Each week, a few more members came back. Each week, the parking lot was a little more full. We were invited to speak at a fireside one evening, and we could hardly believe the size of the ward—it had almost doubled, and there was a sweet spirit that permeated the room. At first the ward didn't even have a pianist; in spite of this, the senior missionary sister suggested they put on a musical. She was initially frightened by the undertaking, but ultimately it was a tremendous success. It was a bonding experience that sweetly pulled the ward members together. The soloists, so excited to perform, felt the Spirit as they sang. The ward was thrilled to think they could do as well as other wards. The bishop told the senior couple they had been a great force for good in his ward. He thanked them for their willing work that helped bring the love of the Lord so richly into his ward.

# Setting an Example of Missionary Service to Others

Senior missionaries feel a bond with the younger missionaries as they work together. They find they become a resource to the younger missionaries, and they are able to help answer questions that investigators have. They have experience that the younger missionaries lack, and are able to see how to easily solve problems that might stop the progress of an investigator toward total conversion. One senior missionary companionship had just such an experience. Two young sister missionaries came to them, greatly concerned about a family they were teaching. "We can't imagine what has happened," said the sisters. "We have been teaching a wonderful family. Everything has been going well. The other day when we arrived for a teaching appointment the father met us at the door with the *Book of Mormon* in his hand and said they did not want to continue meeting with us. We tried to talk to them but they just said they could not continue. We feel so bad. We know they felt the Spirit and they have been so eager to learn about the gospel."

The senior missionary related: "The impression came to me to tell the sisters to call the senior missionary couple in their area to meet with the family. We encouraged the sisters to go by the home often, say hello, and see how the family was doing from time to time. It was a few weeks before a telephone call explained that when the senior couple visited the family they were told the family could not read and the parents were not comfortable discussing it with the younger missionaries. The problem was solved. The family was baptized."

Some senior missionary couples have attributed the

missionary service of their grandchildren to the example they set. Their grandchildren decided to follow the example of their grandparents. One sister said that while she was serving her mission two grandsons had submitted their papers and were awaiting their mission calls. She could not express fully how delighted she was when the boys had a change of heart and were anxiously waiting for their assignments in the mission field. "If you can do it, so can we!" they wrote.

Another couple was struggling with their health after they were in the mission field. It was suggested those senior missionaries return home a little early to deal with their health problems. The missionaries considered the suggestion but felt the problems they were experiencing were insignificant and would still be there even if they were at home. They determined to complete their mission. "We want our grandchildren to know how important it is to serve and complete a full-time mission."

Elder Douglas J. Martin recognized the ongoing work of senior missionaries when he observed: "Whenever I meet and talk with missionary couples, I am filled with love and respect for their humility. . . . They regard their missions as one of the great opportunities to serve the Master in their lives. They always ask, 'How many grandchildren have you?' Our response of eight is quickly overshadowed with 'We have sixteen' or 'twenty-three,' or maybe 'twenty-seven' and almost always with 'And there are two we haven't seen yet.' They miss their family and grandchildren, but they don't complain. Instead, they look forward to that great homecoming reunion. . . . All these missionary couples are finding new purpose and fulfillment in their lives."[5]

# Missionary Service Does Not
# Always Involve a Call

Some of the most valuable missionary service given does not involve a formal call. By constantly looking for ways to support and help the missionary effort numerous avenues avail themselves.

One sister, wanting to contribute to missionary service, volunteered to come into the mission office and do any chore that would be helpful. She had such a happy and cheerful attitude and was always willing to accept a project that needed to be done. She lifted a tremendous load from our mission office staff.

Donating money to help missionaries who might need financial assistance can prove a major blessing in a missionary's life. For example, we had a young missionary whose father died, leaving the family at home in desperate financial straits. His ward rallied to his aid and continued to help his mother and brother at home so he could complete his mission.

Some have assisted by driving missionaries to their appointments. Others have gone through their closets and given good clothing to missionaries coming from underdeveloped countries.

A very sad incident happened in our mission that could have been avoided if only others had cared and served through writing letters. A young missionary arrived to serve. We soon found he had virtually no one at home who cared about him. He had been raised by a grandmother after his parents had abandoned him. As a new missionary he was desperate for someone to whom he could write. While in the

MTC, he had written eighty letters, one to nearly every person he knew. He received only a single reply. That letter asked that he quit writing. My heart broke for this young man. His self-image was so damaged and shaken that he had a difficult time on his mission. If he had had someone, anyone, in his home ward who would have written to encourage him and let him know someone cared, it would have made all the difference.

Each missionary needs someone from the home ward who will write, showing the missionary someone cares that he is giving his time in service to the Lord. Many missionaries notice that after they have been out for several months the volume of mail decreases, even from parents. Supporting missionaries through letters is something every ward member can do. Missionaries love any news from home and are always delighted to receive mail. Letters that communicate faith, happiness, courage, and spiritual experiences are great morale boosters to missionaries. Their own testimonies are strengthened as they hear from ward members who care about them and recognize the importance of the work they are doing. The demand on their time is great; write without expecting a letter in return. It is truly an act of service.

## Many Ways to Serve a Mission

Missionary service comes in many shapes and forms. A dear friend with badly crippled feet has served five missions. She has served a proselyting mission, a temple mission, a family history mission, a visitors' center mission, and a Church service mission. In each, she has been a light to others.

Some older individuals cannot leave home because of

poor health or heavy financial or family responsibilities. Yet there are still opportunities for missionary work. For instance, one can be set apart as a missionary but continue to live at home.

A miracle can be brought about by a conscientious member locator missionary. The Church has missionaries that as part of their mission try to locate members when their records are returned to Church headquarters because the local wards cannot find the members concerned. They may make hundreds of calls a day with only one or two yielding any fruit. But, oh, the miracles their diligent service brings!

One instance happened when a faithful couple had lost track of a grown son who suffered with learning disabilities. Because he did not maintain a constant address or phone number, it was difficult for them to check on him regularly. Then a member locator missionary called and called, refusing to give up, pursuing every possible lead. At last, home teachers in a ward were asked to check out his last known address. They searched and found him living in unhealthy conditions. The home teachers, in turn, went the second mile and helped him get back on his feet. They assisted him in finding a better place to live and helped him find a job managing some apartments, a job well within his capabilities. He began coming to church again. He eventually met a lovely woman and married her in the temple. They, of course, have since been reunited with his joyous parents, and he continues to do well. Just a simple thing like finding the person that goes with a name on a record yielded a changed life. That member locator missionary was a tool in the hand of the Lord to bring one of His lost sheep back to the fold.

# Receiving Blessings of Health and Protection

One lovely couple that served in our mission is a perfect example of having the protection of the Lord over their health. The couple was on their way to an appointment when the elder said that he did not feel well. At once, they both thought it might be a heart attack. The sister was directed to a man on the street who could offer help. He called the paramedics, then stayed with the couple, making the elder as comfortable as possible. The sister called the bishop, who came almost immediately and gave her husband a beautiful blessing. At the hospital the doctors indicated they would not know if he would even be out of danger for at least three days, yet he was released from the hospital in just four days. Later, when doctors in London examined him, they could not believe that he had ever had a heart attack.

His wife told me that her husband's patriarchal blessing said Satan would go to great lengths to break his body in order to break his testimony and stop him from doing the work of the Lord. The Lord was a bulwark of strength against the onslaughts of the destroyer.

Older couples have served well in countries where the weather and the sanitary conditions are difficult. Many are blessed with health and increased vigor to respond to the physical challenges of a mission. They are also given the strength to overcome chronic health problems. One sister missionary laughingly said, "I'd have arthritis at home anyway. I might as well have it here while I'm serving."

## New Experiences, New and Dear Friends

One of the most exciting aspects of serving a mission is having the opportunity to study the scriptures regularly. After a lifetime of study, some senior missionaries are amazed at the depth and insight newly gained when living the missionary schedule of daily scripture study. The scriptures truly are the Lord's words to man and are revealed even more completely while serving in His work.

As one might expect, some of the best friends one will ever have in life will be made while serving a mission. With one great common purpose guiding lives, friendships with other missionaries and members who are also dedicated to spreading the gospel are made and soon cherished. This common bond fosters enduring friendships with people one might not otherwise have the opportunity to know.

Of course, the most pleasant friendships of all are those made with investigators one gently guides into the gospel. The joy of seeing the progress made by these newfound friends is intense and lifelong. The satisfaction is like none other one can have in this mortal life.

## Missionary Service Will Make You Happy

Most of us have spent a lifetime pursuing a career and taking the responsibility for raising a family. We have been busy and preoccupied. But now we have the opportunity to serve the Lord with all our hearts, might, mind, and strength. Our concerns about consecrating our time and means to the Lord can now take flight. Whatever fears you may have of adjusting to a new place or of talking to strangers will vanish as you devote yourselves to missionary work. When you place yourself in the Lord's hands for his use, marvelous things happen. With every challenge comes a blessing. With every struggle comes the lifting of one's spirit. And most of all, with missionary work comes joy. This joy is the true happiness that most people seek all their lives. When you lose yourselves in service, you find the very thing that will make you supremely happy in this life.

## *You Can Do It!*

Speaking of my own days of missionary service and leadership in England, I now know for myself of the love President Gordon B. Hinckley has for that grand country of Great Britain. I better appreciate my progenitor who would not take the easy way, instead choosing to be burned at the stake. I know now of the wondrous children of God who live there, who serve there, and who will serve there. And I know that through such missionary service we can be the instruments to bring to pass the work and the glory of the Lord.

Certainly there are challenges, but his love and blessings become quickly apparent. As we serve we become close to the Lord, closer than ever before. Opportunities come wherein missionaries may participate in missionary miracles as each becomes a trusted ambassador of the Lord Jesus Christ. Whatever doubts you may harbor regarding your ability to fulfill such a mission, that ability is known to God, and as you put your years of dedication and preparation into missionary service you will be abundantly blessed with capacities that exceed your present spiritual level. You will, like those many who have gone before, be part of the noble endeavor of bringing souls unto Christ.

When I was really young I thought life began when I was a teenager; as a teenager I was sure it was when I was old enough to be on my own and make all my own decisions. When I got married, I thought life was just beginning for me. Then when we had our first child and began our family, I thought this was what I'd waited for. Now that my children are grown and have children of their own, I find the world of a grandmother is wonderful. Now, having served in the mission with my husband has taught me that just when I think life may be over, it's just beginning again!

As Elder Neal A. Maxwell stated, "Looking through the lens of gospel perspective, we see more clearly what life is really all about."[6] I have learned that as I have responded to life on gospel terms, my life has been filled with the richness of gospel-refined experiences, and I have come away most happy and most blest. The same will prove true in anyone's life who is obedient to the gospel and rejoices in serving the Master.

# Notes

Lillian S. Alldredge is a graduate of the University of Utah. She is the mother of six children and the grandmother of eight. She has served in many capacities in the Church and recently returned from serving with her husband, who presided over the England London Mission from 1997 to 2000.

1. Sheri L. Dew, *Go Forward With Faith* (Salt Lake City: Deseret Book, 1996), p. 69.
2. Daniel H. Ludlow, ed., *Encyclopedia of Mormonism,* 4 vols. (New York: Macmillan, 1992), 1:231.
3. "Bible, English," in *LDS Bible Dictionary,* p. 624.
4. Thomas S. Monson, "Missionary Memories," *Ensign,* November 1987, p. 43.
5. Douglas J. Martin, "In the Service of the Lord," *Ensign,* November 1987, p. 24.
6. *The Neal A. Maxwell Quote Book,* ed. Cory H. Maxwell (Salt Lake City: Bookcraft, 1997), p. 247.

*Chapter 11*

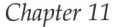

# All Things Are
# Spiritual

**GEORGIA LAUPER GATES**

*"Study and learn . . . good books . . . languages, tongues,*
*and people" D&C 90:15*

The phone rang as Crawford and I were readying our new
Salt Lake City home for the next day's arrival of the moving
van from Wisconsin. To say I was unprepared would be an
understatement indeed. Would I be willing to write a chapter

for a forthcoming book? This was a truly startling proposal to one who has trouble writing out a grocery list!

But as the caller described the project I realized that I had at least one qualification: age! I also have a husband who, though in his eighth decade, is youthful, energetic, and still trying to decide what he will be when he grows up. So I know what it means to be actively engaged in good causes in your senior years. We recently decided to move to Salt Lake City after living for thirty-four years in Beloit, Wisconsin. Definitely not a retirement move, perish the thought! But a move to be closer to some new professional opportunities.

When we moved from Provo to Beloit in 1966, we believed it was for career purposes and that we would be returning to Utah after a few years. What we didn't know then is that the Lord had quite a different agenda for us and that our sojourn in the Midwest would last a third of a century. Beloit is a small industrial community of 35,000 on the border of Wisconsin and Illinois. Having lived for ten years in a booming and bustling ward with a handsome new building in Provo, Utah, we experienced major religious-culture shock when we arrived in Beloit. It was the familiar story of a small branch of the Church, whose services were held on the second floor of a run-down building. The facility was replete with a weekly collection of beer cans and cigarette butts needing to be removed before the meetings began.

The small group of members came considerable distances to meet in these humble circumstances, but they came regularly and served faithfully in the numerous callings held by each one. There was much to learn from these stalwart souls, and far from us bringing the true order of things to them, they blessed our lives in ways we could not have anticipated. As might be expected, any newcomers to the Beloit Branch were greeted with joy and warmth. We were immediately made to feel welcome, and immediately pressed into service, for the Lord's agenda for us was to build up the kingdom in southern Wisconsin.

Aside from three families who had been transplanted from the West, our branch membership was made up of converts. Most of them came from very humble circumstances, but their commitment to the gospel, to the Church, and to their callings was prodigious. In Provo I had not been called as a visiting teacher, and I had rarely been visited. Visiting teaching didn't seem to be much of a priority in that place and time. In the Beloit Branch, however, every active woman was a visiting teacher, and each pair visited their assigned "teachees" regularly. When I was called to be Enid Anderson's companion, I quickly adjusted my former attitude and became a 100 percent visiting teacher. Enid showed the way with her sweet spirit and her determination to rise above the many obstacles in her path.

In addition to the standard visiting teaching callings we had, every active member of the Beloit Branch served in numerous other ways. And I mean major ways! If you were not president of the Relief Society, Young Women, or Primary, you were a counselor, a secretary, or at the very least a teacher. The job pool was small but very concentrated as the few members earnestly labored to provide the full Church program.

It was in these new circumstances that I became acquainted with Ethel Falter, the doyenne of the Beloit Branch. She was born into a large family and grew up on a farm in Northern Wisconsin. She had married, but had no children, was widowed early, and became acquainted with the Church while in her sixties. She was a woman of great determination and self-discipline, and when she was touched by the gospel she made the decision to be baptized despite her fragile health and the fact that the baptism would be taking place out-of-doors in the winter. She recounted this experience with satisfaction, declaring that she had not even caught cold in the freezing weather.

Sister Falter had an innate love and desire for beauty, but her mother had told her early on that, if she wanted to have pretty things, she would have to make them herself. She remembered that as a newlywed she made curtains from pleated funny papers since she could not afford to buy fabric. But when I knew her, much later in her life, she was living in a comfortable home, surrounded by lovely things she had created. The artistic talents she had been born with had been well developed through her life, so that she could sculpt lovely children's heads of clay, paint delicate designs on china, knit beautiful lace with needles as fine as pins, and tat floral decorations for the stationery she used and gave as gifts. In short, she had created a beautiful life for herself and for the many she called friends.

Sister Falter was also very generous in sharing her abilities with others. Anyone who was interested could watch her tat or knit and be taught those techniques from a kindly master. She opened her home to the women of the Church and shared her delicious food and gracious hospitality with many sisters who had not experienced such a style of life before. As evidence of her self-discipline, Sister Falter never slumped in a chair. She sat up with back straight, head erect at all times, since she believed that was the ladylike thing to do. And she was definitely a lady, a lady with a love for the gospel and devotion to the way of life the Savior taught. When the Relief Society Building in Salt Lake City was under construction, she had a great desire to be a part of it. She created an exquisite tablecloth of specially ordered linen and handmade lace, and it was my pleasure to send it to the Relief Society general offices with a short biography of this remarkable lady. She exemplified the words of the thirteenth Article of Faith: "If there is anything virtuous, lovely, or of good report or praiseworthy, we seek after these things."

The inevitable day came when Sister Falter could no longer stay in her home or care for herself. Her friend Ida Bennett, another dear woman of senior age in our branch, took over the details of moving Sister Falter to a small and attractive elder-care home and managing her affairs for the rest of her life. No one asked Ida Bennett to do this, but she saw the need and willingly served her friend and sister in the gospel as long as it was necessary. Ida had not been blessed with the artistic talents of Sister Falter, but she had a wonderfully warm heart and compassionate spirit that directed her to those in need of her own special talents. These she shared generously in her callings as Relief Society president and exemplary visiting teacher. I was fortunate to be Sister Bennett's visiting teaching companion for many years, and there could not have been a more faithful and devoted woman called to the work. She lived by the scriptural injunction in Matthew 25:40, "Inasmuch as ye have done it unto one of the least of these my brethren, ye have done it unto me."

I was blessed to grow up in a musical home. My mother's role was to encourage and produce music, my father's role was to support it. He did this by paying for endless lessons and music for his four daughters and standing back at a safe distance.

My mother was involved in music from her youth and enjoyed the positive influence of an outstanding and inspiring teacher. When she and my dad settled in Oakland, she began to share her musical zeal with the members of Dimond Ward. She organized a women's chorus and embarked on a lifelong activity as music conductor. After a family move to San Francisco, Mother hit her stride by organizing the Sunset Ladies Chorale, a group of women in the Sunset District of San Francisco. Mostly Church members, they loved to sing, and especially loved to sing under the direction of Jean Lauper. She had a way of making music enjoyable and inspiring and was always appreciative and encouraging of the most modest talents.

Mother had an uncanny way of knowing about any new talent that came into the area, and in short order the latest discovery would find herself in the Chorale. Or if the newcomer had superior talent, she would be invited to solo in the next concert. Mother liked nothing better than to nurture and encourage those with special musical gifts. I still have photos taken at a number of the concerts given at the Sunset Ward chapel over a span of many years. Some of the pleasant faces of the singers appeared year after year, a testimony to the loyal and devoted group of women that Mother attracted.

Mother had a unique approach to Church service. She made up her own callings. When I was a teenager the Young Men and Young Women (then MIA) would meet throughout the school year, but would be off in the summer months. Mother had the idea that some kind of fun summer activity would be good to keep the young people in the habit of coming to church. With the approval of the bishop (my dad), the MIA Summer Chorus was born. The young people of the ward were invited to come to a weekly rehearsal of popular songs, familiar music from operettas and musicals, and fun songs. Afterwards there would be a dance to recorded music. At the end of the summer, a concert was given.

The activity was a hit from the beginning and attracted members and nonmembers as well. After some years of conducting the MIA Summer Chorus, Mother decided that with all the talent that had developed she would use the summer months to rehearse and then produce an operetta. The first of these were rather forgettable works such as *Meet Arizona* and *In Gay Havana.* But our family had always had a special fondness for Gilbert and Sullivan, so in the summer of 1951 Mother produced her first G. and S. operetta, *H.M.S. Pinafore.* This was followed the next year by *The Gondoliers.* As in earlier productions, Mother devised an appealing publicity campaign, did the casting, sewed many of the costumes, produced and directed the production, and conducted it! The talent that was assembled in these ward operettas was impressive. Mother didn't restrict herself to ward members or even Church members, if there was someone who could play a given role better. Barbara Eden, who was my high school classmate and friend, made her first dramatic appearance on the Sunset Ward stage. Laurence Guittard went on from the Sunset Ward production of *The Gondoliers* to a distinguished career on Broadway.

In addition to the Ladies Chorale and the ward summer productions, Mother's influence was felt for many years as conductor of an all-city PTA chorus, "The Mothersingers." Her love of music and tremendous drive and enthusiasm for it had a profound effect on many women of San Francisco.

Some women who had no children in the city schools joined the PTA so they could sing in the chorus. Then, as music director for the San Francisco Stake, she not only arranged for the music for years of stake meetings but also created many powerful and inspirational programs on music that involved wards, branches, and individuals. These too brought an extra dimension of beauty and depth to the members of our stake.

In the life of my mother I saw enacted constantly this scripture: "Verily I say, men should be anxiously engaged in a good cause, and do many things of their own free will, and bring to pass much righteousness; for the power is in them, wherein they are agents unto themselves" (D&C 58:27–28).

Being brought up in a home where Church and music were the focus of much of our activity, and with Mother and Dad always at the center of it, gave my sisters and me a unique view of the world. Mother started me on piano lessons when I was five. She told me later that she wanted me to have a skill that would help me socially when I got older, not mentioning that I was plain, shy, and wore thick glasses. Though I liked playing the piano, I hated to practice. I would think of every possible subterfuge to avoid it. Mother would encourage me to practice by offering to do the dishes in my place. This sometimes worked. The piano and I were an off-again on-again affair for many years, for when I wouldn't practice Mother would stop my lessons in exasperation. Then I would spend a lot of time at the piano, and she would think I was ready to learn and would start me again. A benefit of not practicing during the sporadic times I took lessons was that I became a very good sight-reader. I got lots of practice at this because I usually sight-read the music at my piano lessons.

When I was twelve I was called to be the Junior Sunday

School pianist in our ward. This was an experience that made playing the piano pleasant and useful, and I found that I liked it a lot. I had no trouble with the simple children's songs because of my sight-reading experience. The songs were fun and the children sang them enthusiastically, and I knew that no one was listening to me with a critical ear. As time went by I had many opportunities to accompany singers and instrumentalists in church and in school. It was a thrill for me to be considered good enough to accompany the MIA Youth Chorus, some of the Sunset Ward Operettas, the Sunset Ladies Chorale, and even the Mothersingers a few times. My accompaniment experience did far more for me in terms of developing my pianistic and musical abilities than piano lessons ever had. When I went to BYU I was able to earn my spending money by being a hired accompanist to one of the vocal teachers.

Long before that, I realized that I was not a soloist. The many recitals I played in as a child were anticipated with dread and completed with great relief. But I very much enjoyed being at the edge of the spotlight by collaborating with other musicians. And I felt that I was developing and using the pianistic abilities I was blessed with and had begun using in church at the age of twelve. My uncle once said that when you are called to a Church position you get on-the-job training. You don't necessarily have any particular skill for that position, but if you are willing to humble yourself and make an effort you will probably be able to do the job creditably and will have increased your own abilities.

Those early experiences were the beginnings of a lifetime of musical opportunities. Wherever we have lived I have been called on to share my keyboard abilities, and during our time in Beloit I functioned first as the sacrament pianist (in our pre-organ days) and then as the sacrament meeting organist. Also during those years I had a wonderful friend and piano companion with whom I played piano duets. Judy and I became acquainted through a mutual friend and we immediately hit it off both musically and personally. I discovered that performing with another pianist was not at all like performing alone, and I enjoyed immensely the unique association that we had. For over three decades we met together almost weekly, preparing for performances. We were regulars on the local music club programs, and we performed for many civic organizations, retirement homes, and even with the symphony under Crawford's baton. Judy often said, "We're so lucky to have music in our lives!"

I don't want to give the impression that I am a fabulous pianist or organist. I'm really quite average. Perhaps if my twelve-year-old self had not had a positive experience, my musical history would have been quite different. But the chances to use and increase my ability have come to me through my activity in the Church and have enabled me to serve in this enjoyable way throughout my life. "And all this for the benefit of the church of the living God, that every man may improve upon his talent" (D&C 82:18).

Mother was a great reader. Our house was full of books and she loved to read to us bits of books she was currently enthusiastic about. One of our family traditions was that each child received a new book every birthday and Christmas. I can still remember many of the books I received, and I kept some for years. Once I received a small book of Emily Dickinson's poetry that began with the verse "There is no frigate like a book to take us lands away." How wonderful and true that books have such power! When Crawford and I began our family, I wanted the book tradition to continue, and to have books an important part of our children's lives. We established a pattern of bedtime reading that continued through many of the children's classics. I'm happy to say that now our children's children are enjoying the loving and comforting experience of being read to. For "Richer than I you can never be—I had a Mother who read to me."[1] Now when our daughters and daughters-in-law get together, one of their favorite topics of conversation is the newest good books they are reading to their children. "Yea, seek ye out of the best books words of wisdom" (D&C 88:118).

Some years ago a dear and very talented friend, LaVonne Van Orden, began publishing a quarterly newsletter called *Staff Notes.* LaVonne is a musician with a lifetime of experience and service to the Church. She has conducted, accompanied, taught, and written on the subject of music, and the quality of our musical life in the Church is very important to her. She saw a way to extend her musical insights and convictions to others by making them available through the media of print. At her own expense and with her own knowledge of musicians throughout the Church, she started printing and mailing out her publication. The subjects covered were specific suggestions for music in the auxiliaries, to organists, to ward choristers, to choir directors, as well as articles about music in the Church and quotes from General Authorities encouraging music. *Staff Notes* provided a wealth of musical materials that were not readily available elsewhere and were extremely useful to those who were involved in music in the Church. While LaVonne did not seek Church sponsorship for *Staff Notes,* everything included was written and produced from the point of view of a devoted Latter-day Saint. Here again, the use of LaVonne's natural interests and talents has made a tremendous difference to people throughout the Church, many of whom are not even aware of her influence. "Let your words tend to edifying one another" (D&C 136:24).

Recalling LaVonne's great contribution brings me to another subject that can be the culmination of a lifelong interest or ability—being called to use one's talents in missionary service. *Staff Notes* is no longer being published because LaVonne and her husband, Richard, are now serving a mission in Jerusalem. She produces the musical offerings at the Jerusalem Center, and Richard is director of hosting.

Another example of sharing a particular talent through missionary service is Nonie Sorenson. While she and her husband were raising twelve children, Nonie composed and put on many delightful productions that involved her own and many other young people. I had the pleasure of using one of Nonie's productions in a stake women's conference some years ago. It was a most rewarding experience, even though our performance didn't realize all the musical and rhythmic complexities that were part of Nonie's original production. Nonie and husband, Maynard, now spend half the year in Nauvoo, Illinois, where Nonie writes, rehearses, and produces the entertainments that are put on in the evening. The Church has done a marvelous job in developing Nauvoo and restoring its old buildings to their nineteenth-century state. Many missionary couples serve there and "interpret" the activities that went on when Nauvoo was the gathering place for Latter-day Saints. There are demonstrations of early crafts and interesting exhibits to explain how Nauvoo was founded and what went on there. But in order to keep visitors from leaving after one day, it was decided to have some entertainment in the evening. This is where Nonie comes in. When young people are out of school, those who have made it through the auditioning process spend their summers performing in Nonie's productions. But before and after their time in Nauvoo, Nonie uses the senior citizens who are serving as "living history" missionaries. While many of them have never been on stage before, Nonie manages to teach them to act, sing, and even do a little dancing. And they do a terrific job! After each show is over, the participants come outside to greet the audience members as they leave the hall. One performing sister, newly come to "show business," was heard to exclaim, "Paradise can't be any better than this . . . I'm in Heaven now!" "When ye are in the service of your fellow beings ye are only in the service of your God" (Mosiah 2:17).

The examples given here are just a handful of the hundreds and thousands of faithful members who are generously sharing their time, talents, and abilities to further the work of the Church. Since it is something I'm familiar with, I have dwelt heavily on the area of music, but there are myriad other interests that are equally useful. The Church has need of all our talents, whether they be in the arts, teaching, homemaking skills, organizing, managing, working with children, helping in healthcare, or even the gift of friendship. For as we read in Doctrine and Covenants 46:11–12: "All have not every gift given unto them; for there are many gifts, and to every man is given a gift by the Spirit of God . . . that all may be profited thereby."

To use one's God-given gifts to serve him can be the highest order of joy. I expect that he would like nothing less from his children.

# *Notes*

Georgia Lauper Gates is a fourth-generation member of The Church of Jesus Christ of Latter-day Saints. She is the daughter, wife, and mother of bishops. She served for fourteen years as the stake Relief Society president in the Beloit Wisconsin Stake and then the Madison Wisconsin Stake. She and her husband, Crawford, have four children and fifteen grandchildren.

1. Strickland Gillilan, "The Reading Mother," in *Best-Loved Poems of the American People,* sel. Hazel Felleman (New York: Doubleday, 1936), p. 376.

# Chapter 12

## Inherit the Earth

**HELEN WISCOMB**

*"And I have made the earth rich, and behold it is my footstool"*
*D&C 38:17*

In the Doctrine and Covenants, we read this glorious promise from the Lord: "And I hold forth and deign to give unto you greater riches, even a land of promise, a land flowing with milk and honey, upon which there shall be no curse when the Lord cometh; and I will give it unto you for the land of your inheritance, if you seek it with all your hearts. And this shall be my covenant with you, ye shall have it for the land of your inheritance, and for the inheritance of your children forever, while the earth shall stand, and ye shall possess it again in eternity, no more to pass away" (D&C 38:18–20).

Children sing:

> Whenever I hear the song of a bird
> Or look at the blue, blue sky,
> Whenever I feel the rain on my face
> Or the wind as it rushes by,
> Whenever I touch a velvet rose
> Or walk by our lilac tree,
> I'm glad that I live in this beautiful world
> Heavenly Father created for me.
>
> He gave me my eyes that I might see
> The color of butterfly wings.
> He gave me my ears that I might hear
> The magical sound of things.
> He gave me my life, my mind, my heart:
> I thank Him rev'rently
> For all his creations, of which I am part,
> Yes, I know Heav'nly Father loves me.[1]

In-depth study of Genesis, meditation on the above quotation from the Doctrine and Covenants, and empathetic response to the moving words of the children's song—all speak of the marvelous legacy the Lord has prepared for us. This legacy is a divine bequest accompanied with a responsibility. We sisters in our advanced years can: (1) heighten our sensitivity and awareness of the wonders of God's handiwork and their essential spiritual qualities, testifying of a loving Father and his desire to provide abundantly for his children; and (2) help preserve this legacy by our contributions to beautification of the earth, by teaching succeeding generations by example and counsel to appreciate its wonders and to guard against the earth's defacement.

"And God saw every thing that he had made, and, behold, it was very good" (Genesis 1:31). This was in the beginning when God created the heaven and the earth and declared at the conclusion of each step in the six periods of creation that it was good. "And the Lord God took the man [Adam] and put him into the garden of Eden to dress and to keep it" (Genesis 2:15).

Paramount among the instructions given to Adam and Eve was that they should "multiply, and replenish the earth and subdue it" (Moses 2:28). Bishop John H. Vandenberg explained that the commandment to "subdue" intended that Adam should "understand the earth, to use it, to beautify it, to enjoy it." He further stated: "It seems so significant that what God has prepared for us is good. Note especially that everything God has created was given to man with the challenge to subdue it."[2]

Still now, centuries later, the Lord through his chosen prophets continues to instruct us that the earth is good and to underscore our responsibility to advance its goodness. On June 18, 1883, President John Taylor said, "Cultivate the spirit of God . . . beautify Zion and have pleasant habitations, and pleasant gardens and orchards, until Zion shall be the most beautiful place there is on the earth."[3]

In more specific counsel, President David O. McKay said: "There are fences to rebuild, barns to repair, yards to clean up, houses to remodel and to paint, vicious and destructive weeds to destroy as they deface the highway and ravage crops. . . . Let us look around us and see if there is not work near at hand. Such work will be a benefit not only to the individual but to the community and the public generally."[4]

It is wisdom that we should grasp the opportunities, whatever our age and circumstance, to become partners with our Heavenly Father and labor to bless the earth. President Ezra Taft Benson cautioned and reminded us that a resolve to engage in such a good work must translate to deeds: "Some people intend to make a decision and then never get around to it. They intend to paint the barn, to fix the fence, to haul away that old machinery or remove the old shed, but the time of decision just never arrives. . . . The Lord apparently sensed this weakness in His children, for He said: 'Wherefore, if ye believe me, ye will labor while it is called today' (D&C 64:25)."[5]

The Church has been a model for observing the exhortations of its leaders. One of the more conspicuous examples of the Church's advocacy and commitment to this principle occurred in 1997 on the occasion of the sesquicentennial anniversary of the pioneers' entry into the Salt Lake Valley. The First Presidency of the Church declared a "Worldwide Pioneer Heritage Service Day." Appropriately, each ward or branch was asked to donate 150 hours of service to their communities on July 19th. Following are some of the beautification projects completed on that date as reported in the *Church News:*[6]

*Colorado Springs, Colorado:* The three stakes in Colorado Springs worked in cooperation with the city Parks and Recreation Department to clean parks, trails, and right-of-way throughout the city of Colorado Springs and El Paso County.

*Fremont, California:* Some five hundred members of the Fremont, Fremont South, and Hayward California Stakes in northern California donated more than 1,500 hours of service to restore the ancient Ohlones Indian Cemetery in Fremont. Beginning the week before the Church-wide day of service, the extensive clean-up effort culminated on July 19, during which eighteen trees were planted in the cemetery in honor of Ohlones custom of planting to commemorate the cycle of life.

*Alcala De Henares, Spain:* Sixty-five members of the Alcala De Henares Ward of the Madrid Spain Stake gathered litter and other forms of trash in a historic sixteenth-century nature park. Members, ranging in age from two years old to sixty-five years old, filled numerous black trash bags. Members from the Second Ward and Fourth Branch in the stake cleaned graffiti from park benches.

*Auckland, New Zealand:* Members of stakes in Auckland, New Zealand, participated in a variety of service projects. In the Waterview and Mt. Roskill Stakes, workers armed with scythes and spades helped convert Meola Reef from a wasteland into a public preserve. Young Single Adults in the Harbour Stake painted out "tagging," a form of graffiti, on properties in Glenfield, Auckland, New Zealand. And in the Takapuna Ward of that stake, members cleared weeds and washed windows at the North Shore Hospice in Auckland. Two hundred members of the Panmure Stake participated in three projects with the assistance of city officials: cleaning windows and gardens at 300 pensioner apartments; planting native trees at a nature reserve and pulling weeds at the reserve; and cleaning up a roadside.

*Benoni, South Africa:* Members of the Benoni South Africa Stake set a goal of 2,400 service hours, but more than doubled that goal with such projects as fixing up and painting a nursery school, making and donating quilts to a home for the elderly, and teaching skills like cooking and sewing to local women in the community. One such project was done by the Kwa-Thema Branch for the Emmanual Children's Home in Vlakfontein. The branch's Young Women, Relief Society, and priesthood members donated 215 hours of service after discovering the home had no telephone and was in dire need of such basic services as washing clothes, fixing meals, hanging a clothesline, and rehanging doors.

*Frankfurt, Germany:* The Frankfurt Military Ward responded to the call for 150 hours of service by assisting Pastor Leanon Trawick in his ministry to feed the homeless at the Ostpark shelter, one of four shelters he serves in Frankfurt.

The ward Relief Society directed preparation of the lunches of sandwiches, fruit, homemade cookies, and punch by a crew of about twenty-five men and women. About fifty ward members of all ages participated in serving the lunch, singing for the residents and getting to know them.

In these coordinated and organized acts of service and beautification we see that there are many activities besides repairing of barns, fences, house painting, and similar manual labors, labors which may in general be beyond our capacities as sisters. We may think of these as in a sense metaphorical references that do not exclude us from being handmaidens of the Lord, laboring to increase in ourselves and in others an awareness of our inheritance and contributing to beautification of our environment, our lives, and the lives of others in things both temporal and spiritual.

President Brigham Young declared, "The earth is a good earth, the elements are good if we will use them for our own benefit, in truth and righteousness. Then let us be content, and go with our mights to make ourselves healthy, wealthy and beautiful, and preserve ourselves in the best possible manner, and live just as long as we can, and do all the good we can."[7] He further suggested, "Beauty must be sought in the expression of the countenance, combined with neatness and cleanliness and graceful manners."[8] Perhaps in a familiar and fatherly tone, Brother Brigham also said: "Now, sisters, if you will consider these things you will readily see that time is all the capital stock there is on the earth; and you should consider your time golden, it is actually wealth, and, if properly used, it brings that which will add to your comfort, convenience and satisfaction. Let us consider this . . . it is the duty of every man and of every woman to do all that is possible to promote the Kingdom of God on the earth."[9]

In my own associations with children and grandchildren, I have learned of their susceptibility to recognizing and appreciating God's handiwork. In this there exists for us a special opportunity to sustain and enrich their lives with an ever-increasing appreciation of God's earth and the creatures he created for its tenancy.

I am touched in recalling an instance where a young girl approached her mother, smiling and with shining eyes. Her hands were cupped, tenderly confining a wondrous gift she had discovered. She separated her fingers just enough to show her mother the exciting present. What her mother saw may not have thrilled most mothers, as it was a living, light green praying mantis. Together they placed the slender insect on one of the plants in their new garden room. The girl said, "I'm sure as anything he's going to eat up all the white sticky bugs on grandpa's flowering bush."

The child had learned about praying mantises at a family

picnic where she had found one of the unique creatures. Grandma had held it gently, calling attention to its enchanting color and graceful body. She explained that they were harmless to boys and girls and described how the diet of the praying mantis helped to protect beautiful flowers from destructive insects. Grandma told of many of God's creatures like spiders and ladybugs which had been created to eat harmful parasites and were to be thought of as a gift from our Heavenly Father.

In his autobiographical book *A Christmas Memory*, Truman Capote recounts impressions received as a young man through a companionship with an old cousin, Miss Sook Falk, whom he refers to as his "friend." An annual Christmas gift from his friend was a kite. On one occasion she says, "Buddy, the wind is blowing." Then Capote writes:

> The wind is blowing and nothing will do till we've run to a pasture below the house. . . . There, plunging through the healthy waist-high grass, we unreel our kites, feel the twitching at the string like sky fish as they swim into the wind. Satisfied, sun-warmed, we sprawl in the grass and peel satsumas and watch our kites cavort. Soon I forget the socks and hand-me-down sweater. I'm as happy as if we'd already won the fifty-thousand-dollar Grand Prize. . . .
>
> . . . "My, how foolish I am!" my friend cries, suddenly alert, like a woman remembering too late she has biscuits in the oven. "You know what I've always thought?" she asks in a tone of discovery, and not smiling at me but a point beyond. "I've always thought a body would have to be sick and dying before they saw the Lord. And I imagined that when He came it would be like looking at the Baptist window: pretty as colored glass with the sun pouring through, such a shine you don't know it's get-

ting dark. And it's been a comfort: to think of that shine taking away all the spooky feeling. But I'll wager it never happens. *I'll wager at the very end a body realizes the Lord has already shown Himself. That things as they are"*—her hand *circles in a gesture that gathers clouds and kites and grass. . . .*— "just what they've always seen, was seeing Him. As for me, I could leave the world with today in my eyes."[10]

Many of the great men of this dispensation attest to the benefits of exemplary conduct and discipline of an adult. This is well illustrated in the account given by President Spencer W. Kimball of the influences of his father:

> Andrew (Spencer's father) exacted precision from his sons. Pointing to a piece of carpentry such as a cedar toolchest or a corner cupboard, he would say to his second son, "Del, people won't ask how long it required to make the chest or build the cupboard, but how well it was done." A meticulous dresser, Andrew expected the same neatness about the farm. Spencer was taught to soap and oil the harness, hang the collar and bridle and blinds just in place on pegs in the harness shop. The surrey had to be washed, greased, painted. "Too frequently to suit me," remembered Spencer. "Why wash the buggy?" he would moan. "It will just get dusty the first mile out anyhow." But for Father it had to be clean. For Father the hairline of trim paint on the buggy had to be flawless. The fences had to be whitewashed, the trellis painted green, the barn, the granary, the harness shed, all painted. "Sometimes I did not mind work," Spencer recalled. "But looking back, I'm sure my folks must have felt that I was always tired or lazy."[11]

Like the wise grandmother with the praying mantis, Truman Capote's friend, and President Kimball's devoted father, we too can be understanding, loving companions in the lives of the young, asserting a special influence, a special touch as we have, we hope, become endowed with a measure of wisdom during our accumulated years.

## I LOVE TO GO TO GRANDMA'S

*I love to go to Grandma's.*
    *We walk and talk and sing.*
*Sometimes we plant tiny seeds—*
    *We do that when it's spring.*

*We sing about a wee brown thrush,*
    *About the blue, blue sky.*
*When grass is dry we often sit*
    *And watch the clouds float by.*

*I love to go to Grandma's.*
    *In the garden I find buts*
*And snails, and I get dirty;*
    *Still she gives me hugs.*

*I love to go to Grandma's.*
    *It makes her happy when I come.*
*We eat green apples or red grapes,*
    *Sometimes a purple plum.*

*We draw pictures of them, too,*
    *Or sew flowers with colored floss.*
*We play with dominoes or jacks.*
    *She lets me be the boss.*

*She lets me tell her stories*
    *And talk of all my wishes.*
*She listens to me mostly when*
    *Together we do dishes.*

*I guess one thing that I like best:*
*I don't ever have to worry*
*About being slow or wasting time.*
*Grandma's never in a hurry.*[12]

There are many written testaments of how a single experience or incident in the life of a child can make an indelible impression. Knowing this, we sisters, married or single, agile or bedridden, can seek and find opportunities to provide that experience or incident.

While watching a nature program I learned of an amazing phenomenon. It is that the collective motion created by migrating butterflies can influence weather patterns hundreds of miles away. It is encouraging to consider the positive effect, the phenomenon we "twilight" sisters can be if we do not weary in partnering with the Lord to teach young children to love the land, to protect it from clutter, despoilment, and unnecessary depletion. Such should be considered a continuing and vital responsibility during our mortal sojourn on the earth.

For me, art has been both a profession and an avocation. Through its pursuit, the appreciation of an awareness of beauty has been continually nurtured. Growth in this and other areas can be facilitated by the freedom from chores incident to motherhood, employment, and other demands during the earlier years of our lives. Continuing education opportunities abound. Many states provide such for seniors at modest tuition rates. Over a period of several years, my alma mater has enabled me to participate in such programs. After turning sixty, I accumulated many hours in a variety of art classes, which allowed me to improve and retain the ability to create art in various forms. These efforts have permitted me to encourage creativity and to teach both adults and young people in my home. It has been gratifying and rewarding to see several of the younger students, some starting with me as early as age seven, continue on through high school, subsequently receiving art scholarships and ultimately pursuing some facet of art as professionals.

A quotation attributed to Ralph Waldo Emerson provides a provocative set of criteria for successful living: "To laugh often and much; to win respect of intelligent people and the affection of children; to earn the appreciation of honest critics and to endure the betrayal of false friends; to appreciate beauty; to find the best in others; to leave the world a bit better whether by a healthy child, a garden patch, or a redeemed social condition; to know even one life has breathed easier because you have lived. This is to have succeeded."[13]

To this I would add a familiar saying with its implicit challenge and promise: We are never too old to learn, to grow, and to bless the earth and the world within the sphere of our influence. An effort to do so can be a crown of success, placing us in harmony with the divine Father's purposes to preserve the earth as our eternal inheritance.

# Notes

Helen Wiscomb served on the editorial board of the *Children's Friend* and on three writing curriculum committees for The Church of Jesus Christ of Latter-day Saints, writing lessons for Young Women, Aaronic Priesthood, and Relief Society. For nearly eight years she was a columnist for the *Salt Lake Tribune*.

1. Clara W. McMaster, "My Heavenly Father Loves Me," *Children's Songbook* (Salt Lake City: The Church of Jesus Christ of Latter-day Saints, 1989), p. 228.
2. John H. Vandenberg, "It Was Good," *BYU Speeches of the Year*, December 8, 1964, p. 3.
3. John Taylor, in *Journal of Discourses*, 24:201.

4. David O. McKay, in Conference Report, April 1938, pp. 16–21.

5. Ezra Taft Benson, "This Life Is the Time," *Church News*, September 22, 1990.

6. "Worldwide Pioneer Heritage Service Day," *Church News*, July 26, 1997.

7. John A. Widtsoe, ed., *Discourses of Brigham Young*, Deseret Book Company, Salt Lake City, 1966, p. 302.

8. Ibid, p. 214.

9. Ibid.

10. Truman Capote, *A Christmas Memory* (New York: Alfred A. Knopf, 1989).

11. Spencer W. Kimball, *A Small Boy in a Small Town*, ed. Edward L. Kimball and Andrew E. Kimball, Jr. (Salt Lake City: Bookcraft, 1977), pp. 28–29.

12. Poem by the author, Helen Wiscomb.

13. Quotation obtained from a website, GeoCities, in response to inquiry for references on "Success." Quotation is attributed to Ralph Waldo Emerson but has not been documented as originating with him.

# Chapter 13

# The Things of a Better World

## CAROLYN J. RASMUS

*"Lay aside the things of this world, and seek for the things of a better" D&C 25:10*

Lists! They'd become as much a part of my life as eating and sleeping. Daily I made lists of what I needed to do. I made lists of things I needed to do as the Relief Society president or when I served as chairman of a committee. And of course, there was the constant task of rewriting it onto the next day's list when everything that was supposed to be done didn't get completed on that day. It's funny: As I look back over my life, I can't remember any list that I actually generated. All my lists were things that came as a result of my job or a calling or my role as a family member or a house owner.

I don't remember ever really disliking making these lists. It seemed a natural thing for me. I've always loved pens and pencils and paper. I've collected every kind of pen that's been made and have tried every size and type of calendar and planner invented. Mostly this is because I love to keep track of things, to write them down. I became aware that my list making was a bit obsessive when I realized that I was adding things to my lists that I'd already done, but hadn't previously written down, just so I would have the pleasure of crossing them off!

As I contemplated retiring from full-time teaching, it occurred to me that my list-making habits would change dramatically. In fact, at one point I began to wonder what kind of lists I'd even make if no one or no something (like a job) dictated what things needed to be done.

But as I neared the date of my retirement, everyone I talked with wanted to know, "What are you going to do?" "Where are you planning to travel?" I was tempted to respond: "I'm not going to do anything; I'm not going to go anywhere except home!" In fact, one day I did. But I kept being pushed. "Oh, sure; what big plans do you really have?" or "You must be planning on going somewhere exciting." And so, once again, I resorted to making a list of the things I would do during retirement.

As a seasoned list maker, I even identified the things I

would accomplish during the first year of my retirement. And oh, they were grand! The list included: index all my personal journals (the fourteen bound ones and "numerous" files of loose papers), write *and* publish a book, write my personal history, organize and annotate photographs (more than forty years' worth!), take a gardening class, learn to scan pictures and other documents, organize and type favorite quotations onto a zip drive, take a drawing class, memorize all the scripture mastery scriptures, learn to play the piano well enough to accompany hymns in church . . . ad nauseam.

Well, it's been just about a year since I retired. Not long ago I reviewed the list I'd made. I have not completed one single thing! No check marks, no nothing. In fact, I haven't even started on any of the things I thought I'd have completed by now. I realize that this could be a perfect setup for feelings of guilt or at least a good case of anxiety. Why was I experiencing neither? Questions and self-doubts began to fill my mind: Was I no longer goal oriented? Was I just getting lazy? Maybe I wasn't self-motivated enough to accomplish anything on my own. Did I need the structure of a job or motivation from others to accomplish anything?

Several things came quickly to mind. First, I realized that I really didn't feel bad about not having even attempted to start what had seemed important enough to be placed "on the list." As I reflected over the past year I remembered moments of great peace and satisfaction—even joy. I had been so excited about having the time to do dry-pack canning for myself and for others who were working and couldn't go to the cannery during the day. I will forever hold dear the time I was able to sit with a ward sister during the final weeks and days of her life. What fun I'd had helping a young teenage woman learn to read recipes and cook when her mother experienced a broken ankle! What a delight, on a chance meeting in the mall, to have the time to sit and visit with an older sister in my stake. For someone like me, who has never had children, what a sweet and calming experience to regularly hold one of the triplets born to a neighbor-friend.

At an earlier time in my life all of those things would have seemed insignificant—each just one more thing I "needed to do" in an already busy day. But somehow, growing older enables us to see things from a different perspective. What I would have at one time called "little things" now seem to be those of most importance. I have been reminded of something that Mother Teresa wrote. When younger, I sensed it was right; but now I recognize the wisdom of what she taught.

> We must not drift away from the humble works, because these are the works nobody will do. It is never too small. We are so small that we look at things in a small way. But God, being Almighty, sees everything great. Therefore, even if you write a letter for a blind man or you just go and sit and listen, or you take the mail for him, or you visit somebody or bring a flower to somebody—small things—or wash clothes for somebody, or clean the house. Very humble work, that is where you and I must be. For there are many people who can do big things. But there are very few people who will do the small things.[1]

Somehow, I think Mother Teresa understood what the Lord meant when he counseled Emma Smith to "lay aside the things of this world, and seek for the things of a better" (D&C 25:10).

I found myself pondering this verse. I recalled that President Gordon B. Hinckley had used this section of the

Doctrine and Covenants as a text for a general women's meeting address. He noted, "Insofar as I know, this is the only revelation given specifically to a woman." He then read the concluding words of the Lord to Emma, "This is my voice unto all" (D&C 25:16), and added, "Therefore, the counsel given by the Lord on this occasion is applicable to each of you." He spoke of a letter he had received from a woman who, with a great sense of frustration, indicated that she had been defeated or failed in most of what she had tried to do. She asked him, "What does God expect of me?" President Hinckley replied, "Some of the things which God expects of her and of every other woman—in fact, each of us—are set forth in this beautiful revelation."

He discussed each verse, not only as it pertained to Emma but also in terms of what counsel it holds for us today. I scanned quickly to his commentary on verse 10. "I feel," President Hinckley said, "he was not telling Emma that she should not feel concerned about a place to live, food on her table, and clothing. He was saying to her that she should not be obsessed with these things, as so many of us are wont to be. He was telling her to get her thoughts on the higher things of life, the things of righteousness and goodness, matters of charity and love for others, the things of eternity."[2]

Now there was a sobering thought. I immediately thought of how "obsessed" (President Hinckley's word!) I'd been about so many of the things I'd written on years' worth of lists. Then I reflected on the activities of this past year. I began to wonder if I might finally be beginning to "lay aside the things of this world."

I went to my journal to reread something I'd written following my mother's death earlier in the year. It's interesting to note that the entry began with Doctrine and Covenants 25:10:

> Personal experiences of the past 5 months have made me increasingly aware of the need to "lay aside the things of this world, and seek for the things of a better."
>
> My 94-year-old Mother experienced a steady decline in health since this past Christmas. My phone calls increased to daily visits; I made 4 trips to Ohio to spend time with her.
>
> Though not a Latter-day Saint, my mother was a woman of faith and an active member of the Lutheran Church. Early last month, as she lay in the hospital, we talked openly about her approaching death. Mentally alert and delightful, she picked out the dress she wanted to wear and gave me instructions to have it cleaned. Then she remembered she had no shoes that matched. I assured her that where she was going she wouldn't need them.
>
> I rushed back to Utah to fulfill teaching and speaking assignments, but after completing a speaking assignment in Idaho I felt impressed that I should return to Ohio as soon as possible. I arrived the next evening.
>
> Mother was no longer able to speak, but the look of her clear, blue eyes told me she was as alert as ever. We would have just 6 days together before she died.
>
> There was no question in my mind that I had been prompted to return. Suddenly, meetings that I felt I *couldn't* miss seemed insignificant. Isn't it interesting how experiences which place us so close to the veil (birth, death, and eternal marriage) have the power to cause us to change our schedules and deadlines and literally put aside the things of this world? I found the rushing pace of daily life slowed immensely as I sat hour after hour by her bed—holding her hand or rubbing her legs. Since she couldn't respond to anything I did or said, I found myself

constantly praying to know what to share or read, what to do, and when it was important to remain silent. I felt totally dependent on the Lord.

Daily we held a devotional. I would pray, read from the scriptures, share a personal experience or story, and read more scriptures. I found increasing peace and comfort as we worked our way through the Psalms, feeling that many had been written just for us in this particular circumstance.

When Mother was no longer able or wanting to take food, I chopped ice and placed it in her mouth. By Thursday evening she could no longer swallow. I was surprised to hear myself saying, "If I were you I would want to know what is happening to me. You have only 2 or 3 days to live." Then in my non-medical way I told her how her body would begin to be less and less efficient; to literally shut down. "It's a natural process," I told her. Nothing to be frightened about. She looked at me knowingly and peacefully.

I stayed until about 2 A.M. on Saturday. Three of her caregivers came to me. They had been crying. One spoke for all. "We know you are a religious woman. Could we kneel around your mother's bed and would you offer a prayer?" We knelt together and I offered one of the most sincere and heartfelt prayers of my life.

Sunday morning, Mother's breathing was increasingly labored. I sought divine guidance to know what to do or say. Then, almost instinctively, I found myself turning to the scriptures. Without any forethought, I was led to four scriptures. I read to Mother from 2 Timothy 4:6–8, suggesting that she like Paul had "fought a good fight" and "finished [her] course," having "kept the faith." Next, I turned to 2 Timothy 1:1–7, confirming that she had "unfeigned faith" like Lois and Eunice. Although I am familiar with these scriptures, I had not read them recently, nor even thought of them in relation to Mother. I felt guided by the Spirit to turn to 1 John 4:18–19 and read, "There is no fear in love; but perfect love casteth out fear. . . . We love him, because he first loved us." Thinking of all Mother had taught me, through word and example, I found myself turning to 3 John 1:4. "I hope," I said, "that you have joy, knowing that your children are seeking to 'walk in truth.' " It was more of a question than a statement.

As her breathing became more labored I wanted with all my heart to be able to do something to make it easier. I knelt by her bed and cried and cried. "I'm going to miss you," I said. "I want to help you, but there isn't anything I can do," I said. Then the impression: "Yes there is. You can pray." Through tears, I told Heavenly Father that Mother was ready to return to him; of the goodness of her life; of our desire to have his will manifest. Within five minutes, she took her last breath.

It's been interesting to think about the counsel given in Doctrine and Covenants 25:10 in light of these events. How quickly things of the world paled. How scriptures seemed the only appropriate reading material in the last days. How constantly I sought divine guidance, and how instinctive and natural it seemed to pray.

I know these are the things for which we are commanded to seek—the things of a better world. When nothing else will satisfy, there is the word of God, the inspiration of the Holy Ghost, and the gift of prayer—communication with our Heavenly Father, who knows us and loves us.

When we are discouraged, uncertain, overwhelmed, anxious, confused, or feeling inadequate, we can turn to the true sources of strength and power. Increasingly, we can "lay aside the things of this world, and seek for the things of a better." As we do this, I believe the things of this world will indeed be better.

This past year has taught me many lessons I would not have been ready to learn at an earlier age. Lessons of life that come with increasing years come in quiet, often solitary ways. I've experienced them as I've planted flowers and reflected on the beauties of creation. I understand better the condescension of Christ when I hold a tiny baby in my arms and remember that the Creator of this world came as a helpless baby, unknown to most for who he was and what he would do for mankind. I recognize the significance and power of the Atonement as I see charity replace years of anger and feelings of disappointment. As I recognize that I am now the oldest in my family and that I have lived longer than I will yet live, I come to an increasing sense of the need for mercy and forgiveness.

Perhaps the physical body slows and tires a bit more quickly so that we might have increased time to ponder and reflect and meditate. How interesting that when these words are used in the scriptures, invariably they are followed with the description of a vision. This happened to the young Joseph Smith as he "reflected" on the Bible scripture that initiated his visit to the grove we now call sacred (see JS—H 1:11–17), and to Nephi as he sought to see and hear and know the things his father saw in a vision, for following his "pondering" he was blessed to see and know all and more that had been revealed to his father (see 1 Nephi 10:17; 11:1). Likewise, President Joseph F. Smith received a vision concerning the Savior's visit to the spirits of the dead after he "pondered" and "reflected" on the writings in 1 Peter 3 and 4 (see D&C 138).

Now, I don't spend large amounts of time pondering, but

I do find myself giving deeper thought to things that are more eternal than temporal. Does it mean I will never make lists or set goals for the future? No. I think instead I am putting aside more of my own lists and increasing my desire to know what the Lord would have me do, wanting my lists to be more like his lists.

I find it increasingly important to begin each day with "listening" prayer: Who might need my help? What are the most important things I should be about at this particular time? I think of Brigham Young's counsel, "Did you pray . . . this morning? 'No.' 'Why?' 'I was in too much of a hurry.' Stop! Wait!" Then the prophet's counsel, "When you get up in the morning, before you suffer yourselves to eat one mouthful of food . . . bow down before the Lord, ask him to forgive your sins, and protect you through the day, to preserve you from temptation and all evil, *to guide your steps aright, that you may do something that day that shall be beneficial to the Kingdom of God on the earth.*"[3]

Perhaps as I listen more carefully, one day at a time, I will learn to "lay aside the things of this world, and seek for the things of a better."

# *Notes*

Carolyn J. Rasmus joined The Church of Jesus Christ of Latter-day Saints while attending Brigham Young University. After earning her doctorate degree, she served as executive assistant to BYU Presidents Dallin H. Oaks and Jeffrey R. Holland. She also taught at Iowa State University, on Long Island, New York, and at the Orem Institute of Religion. Sister Rasmus has served on the Young Women general board and was administrative assistant to the Young Women general presidency for ten years. She serves on the boards of directors of Deseret Book Company and the Utah County United Way. She is the author of *In the Strength of the Lord I Can Do All Things*, as well as several talks on cassette.

1. *Love: A Fruit Always in Season, Daily Meditations from Mother Teresa* (San Francisco: Ignatius Press, 1987), p. 26.
2. Gordon B. Hinckley, "If Thou Art Faithful," *Ensign*, November 1984, pp. 89–92.
3. Brigham Young, in *Journal of Discourses*, 15:36; emphasis added.

# Chapter 14

## Glorious Eve

### BARBARA B. SMITH

*"Among . . . the righteous . . . our glorious Mother Eve, . . . with many of her faithful daughters" D&C 138:38–39*

Eve is arguably the most storied of all women—maybe because, in one sense, she is "all women." She is the everywoman who stands for all, the symbol of her gender. Our lives as women began with Eve. As we enter a new century of time, a new chapter, another book, we wonder what there is left to say about her. After so many others have written, what prompts me to write yet another line? In answer: I write not so much for what I have to say about Eve as for what she has to say to me, a Latter-day Saint woman mid-stride in life and beyond.

Though scriptural references to her are few, I search them, believing that in finding her I find something of myself and the beginning of what is womanly. I look for the promise and potential of woman that Heavenly Father intended from the beginning. For women, Eve is mother, model, and mentor. She has lived through Eden and the rigors of earth life, and has been crowned with a heavenly glory. Through her life, as it can be found in scripture, we'll seek to learn what she knew that will be helpful to us, especially those of us who have lived long enough to know some of the questions to ask. In a book relating to women past fifty she can become a kind of light set on a hill.

We're searching for what is the "essence of Eve"—what is essentially her. The accounts relating events in the Garden of Eden read, "And Adam called his wife's name Eve," followed by the carefully chosen words, "because she was the mother of all living" (Genesis 3:20; Moses 4:26). Had those words been "the mother of all *the* living," Eve's role might have been focused, at least by definition, far more narrowly to that of giving birth and whatever is related directly to that. But the words given in the scripture are "mother of *all living*"; these suggest that Eve's is the very inclusive role of nurturing life. It is a stretch of mind to try grasping the full meaning of such a calling, but that *she* did understand and fulfill her role is evident in the fact that "our glorious Mother Eve" was among the great ones who appeared in the 1918 vision of Joseph F. Smith (see D&C 138:39).

*This may be the first thing to know about Eve: she is Mother.* Note, this is not quite the same as to say she is *a* mother. A mother is singular and at the same time particular. Eve was called mother before she was mother of a child. Before she and Adam had sons and daughters, she was the "mother of all living." As women we each are mother—whether we claim or reject the title, whether or not we are working toward this as an ideal—I believe it is the birthright of a woman.

We have all known persons who fit our image of mother. Possibly we have seen some we do not know but who fit the image. It may be in a shopping mall, a child is crying or lost or has fallen, and before there is time to look for a parent there is some "mother" picking him up, or drying the child's tears, or giving a hand to hold. This person may not even have a child or a husband or a home, but she is still being mother. Although mothering requires a very knowing person, anyone who really wants to can learn it, though I cannot think of a single place where it is formally taught. She may be a mother of children, but very likely her "covey" or "brood" will not be limited to those to whom she has given birth.

Such mothering is not given only to children (although children are always in need of someone to be their mother), but mothering can be given to parents, or to husbands, or to the next person one sees who needs someone to care who will care more about them at that moment than about herself. You must know someone as I do who always seems to be on her way to the care center with some flowers from her garden. Or there is the unmarried woman who happens to have in her pocket some finger puppets when the child sitting on the next row becomes fretful in church. This kind of person can sometimes be called selfless because she does not appear to be worried about herself, yet she is very conscious of another's need, even though that need may be unspoken.

The good thing is that one can become this kind of person at any age. For some, being past fifty may be the optimal time to start acquiring caring traits, for it is then one has enough control over time to look up from pressing duties. One has the feeling that Heavenly Father looks with appreciation on such persons. If only there were enough people of this kind in the world, we would all fare better.

The possibilities of this special kind of mothering are unlimited and usually unexpected; they touch many facets of a woman's life. For example, Eve learned that her husband was to have "the say" in their family, as told through the words, "thy desire shall be to thy husband, and he shall rule over thee" (Moses 4:22). We do not know her reaction. A wife might be disappointed or even resentful of such an arrangement, but I think Eve was neither of these. The directive was given by the Lord for a good reason (even if that reason may not have been immediately apparent), and I think she accepted it in this way, and not as punishment.

*Of the things we learn from Eve, surely there will be something of faith.* We can see in her acceptance of His direction Eve's remarkable trust in the Lord. She was a "first" in so many ways. Had we, in our day, received that same directive, we would immediately understand that Adam had been given a priesthood role of leadership. But from what we find in the record in Moses and Genesis, there was no mention of "priesthood" but only of "rule." Eve had never had an earthly father who held the priesthood, she had not had a twelve-year-old son whom she had helped rear and prepare to be a holder of the Aaronic Priesthood, yet when told that Adam would rule over her, she trusted the Lord. Today we understand priesthood direction and delegated authority, but Eve's experience was in the beginning. Without the benefit of a history of Church leadership to help her, she had faith enough to accept and to follow that direction.

We don't know how much Mary, the mother of Jesus, knew about Eve. I think Eve has served as mentor for all women. But I could not help thinking how that same trust we saw in Eve was evidenced again when Mary had to trust in the goodness of God to assure her that she was, indeed, to be the mother of his Son. We could see in Mary, too, that quality of mothering the Lord must have known was there in order to have entrusted to her care his Only Begotten.

For another special mother we look to Sister Marjorie Hinckley, the "mother" of the Church in this day. In our minds and hearts we often equate Sister Hinckley with stories of faith. She is not only the wife of our prophet but also has come from a family with a long history of faithful Church members. I think of her when hearing this passage from 2 Timothy: "When I call to remembrance the unfeigned faith that is in thee, which dwelt first in thy grandmother Lois, and thy mother Eunice; and I am persuaded that [is] in thee also" (2 Timothy 1:5). They are people of faith who have made a difference to the history of the Church, people who crossed the plains by wagon, sacrificed and suffered greatly because they would not leave, to suffer alone, a struggling handcart company that had been delayed by heavy snows. We have been inspired by hearing of Sister Hinckley's faithful pioneer family; we also admire Sister Hinckley herself, for herself. Her buoyant belief in the power of doing right and her positive attitude radiate and lift others though her life has been a strenuous one of rearing a sizable family and supporting her husband in his weighty leadership roles that have increased all the years of her married life. Now, at the time when they might be expected to have less strength, the responsibilities are even weightier. Not only does she give her prophet husband the support he needs to meet his extraordinary speaking schedule (which means so much to all the Church); most places he goes, she is at his side as an example of vibrant, stimulating living for women. She and her pioneer ancestors have all had the faith to follow the Lord.

These noble sisters are witness that it matters not so much what your circumstances are or the era in which you live; if you have trust enough you will be found among those of the Lord's faithful.

*To her faith Eve added knowledge.* Eve trusted in the Lord when he announced that in her companionship with Adam "he shall rule over thee." Along with her trust that it was right because it was the Lord who said it, Eve could also see in this arrangement a possible expression for her role to nurture Adam in his position. She saw the need for Adam to be skillful in the way he "ruled over," and the way he responded to her "desires," knowing this could make a major difference in their home, creating either harmony or discord. She could see it was good for one to lead and the other to nurture.

I believe Eve acted according to her faith, but had she only her reason to guide her, hers would have been a reasonable position. As the calming, caring mother over life in the home, Eve could see this position—which gave Adam opportunity to develop his skills as a leader and her the chance to nurture the godlike in him—as very reasonable, that having both lead could foster discord between them. Clearly, it was the position of greater advantage to them both, one that would foster harmony in their home and love in their relationship.

Revealed truth concerning eternal life teaches us to look at life with a long view. We have little time, however, to simply "look at life," for our teaching is of eternal progress. Not only do we believe in living eternally, but we have an ever-present need for becoming—becoming better each day, whatever our age.

The scripture describing our glorious Mother Eve and many of her faithful daughters who lived through the years and served the living God brings to my mind groups of Relief Society sisters who serve so faithfully throughout the Church. Over many years, I traveled to the stakes and regions, and wherever I went found beautifully appointed meetings and faithful sisters carrying out the programs of the Church.

I have always found it refreshing to go into a room full of Relief Society sisters, all ages meeting together, each woman having something to offer the others. The younger women of today who are so progressive, so talented, know they are needed; the older women who have proven themselves share what they have learned through experience while at the same time arc willing to learn from others. For almost as long as the Church has been organized, Relief Society has given women an opportunity for "becoming." With classes for learning and service needs for giving, it is a fertile growing medium for the women of the Church. In the long continuum of life, each woman is on an individual quest for wholeness (or perfection) but is also committed to doing all she can to help others succeed in that same pursuit. There is much of Mother Eve in that commitment.

When searching the scriptures we read "glorious Mother Eve," and wonder how she achieved this stature. We're led to believe it was through good works. For among the last things we read before she is in the gathering of the righteous is in Moses 5:1, "And it came to pass that after I, the Lord God, had driven them out [of the Garden of Eden], that Adam began to till the earth, and to have dominion over all the beasts of the field, and to eat his bread by the sweat of his brow, as I the Lord had commanded him. And Eve, also, his wife, did labor with him."

The description here of Adam and his work is given in almost the very words spoken to him by the Lord when he was sent from the Garden. Eve also received some difficult challenges, by way of reprimand, but they were not these. She was not told to labor in the fields, yet she was nonetheless doing this. We are not given to know her intent, but her working with Adam is so like what Heavenly Father taught (and what we learned by way of Moses): "This is my work and my glory—to bring to pass the immortality and eternal life of man" (Moses 1:39). In this case, her work was helping Adam to succeed on the land as the Lord had commanded.

*Eve teaches us that to help others is womanly.* Some might feel that Eve's working in the field alongside Adam was not a woman's job. This would only be the "some" who have not known the joy of working together as a family, and the opportunity to help one another, even if the work is in the field. I think we may not know all the circumstances for Adam and Eve at this time. I believe what we are seeing is someone helping; Eve would have felt this to be most appropriate work as a helpmate to her husband. Her life as we have found it in the scripture seems consistent with this. Helping another is very much her way, woman's way.

After their chastisement by the Lord, Adam and Eve were strictly obedient (one of the consequences of their eating the forbidden fruit was coming to know good and evil). They seemed to have another order of understanding and obedience after this. They carefully kept each commandment the Lord gave them and heeded all his counsel. Accordingly they had sons and daughters, learned to sacrifice, to repent, and to pray in the name of the Son. Adam received the Holy Ghost and began to prophesy.

"And Adam and Eve, his wife, called upon the name of the Lord, and they heard the voice of the Lord from the way toward the Garden of Eden, speaking unto them and they saw him not; for they were shut out from his presence" (Moses 5:4). There are comparatively few passages of scripture devoted in any way to Eve, which makes each one seem a gem—and, like a gem, faceted. In an effort to appreciate this passage fully, I have tried to turn it, word by precious word, to the light, hoping to see its fullest meaning.

*Adam and Eve pray together.* The first thing we notice is their "togetherness." It is all "Adam and Eve, they . . ." This seems a change from the days in the Garden, where they were more often by themselves. We haven't much proof of this except in the matter of the fruit. And the most telling thing about that is the fact that Satan didn't have difficulty in getting to Adam and Eve separately. For an open space (a garden), without walls, they must have been at some distance apart, because neither Adam nor Eve seemed aware of the other's conversation.

Seen in this present verse, almost by contrast, is their distance from the Lord. But a short while before they could speak to him in person; now he was only a name and a voice: "they called upon the name"; "they heard the voice"; "they saw him not"; " they were shut out from his presence." Their need for one another was doubtless greater because of the loss they felt.

We have considered nearly all the words of this verse and what they can mean, but beyond the words there is feeling communicated: it is Adam and Eve's sense of loss. Without having had the experience, it would be hard to appreciate how great their loss was and how hard to bear. Without that understanding, any comment might be unfair. However, having said that, I will still venture to comment with the suggestion that the closeness of Adam and Eve, evident in their relationship now as apparently lacking before, is certainly some kind of compensation. Especially this is true with (1) the promise they have that through the atoning sacrifice of our Redeemer they can one day work back to where they once were, in the presence of the Father and the Son; and (2) the quality of their relationship being of utmost importance in their gaining that presence once more.

When Adam and Eve called upon the name of the Lord, they received commandments in answer to their prayers. The one other place I can think of commandments being given as a special kind of reply is in Doctrine and Covenants 59:4: "And they shall also be crowned with blessings from above, yea, and with commandments not a few, and with revelations in their time—they that are faithful and diligent before me."

I have to think this was a very tender time for the Lord as well as for Adam and Eve. Just a short while before this they could speak face to face. He couldn't have been any happier about their leaving than they were. He was still so close that they could hear his voice—in the Garden. They must have clung to every word they heard. What he told them was what they *had to do* to get back to his presence. Maybe that is why they called his words *commandments.* I wonder how our lives would differ if we considered, and maybe even called, the answers to prayer we receive "commandments." It does give us something to ponder.

The commandments mentioned in answer to Adam and Eve's prayer were to worship the Lord and to sacrifice.

*To have the essence of Eve we need to remember this about her, that she "heard all these things and was glad"* (Moses 5:11). She was glad about the gospel and the promise of their redemption and resurrection. They were especially happy because of their children, and they taught them the plan of redemption. They were told that if they were obedient, they could have all the blessings promised to the faithful.

So much of the happiness we know comes from our children. This is never more evident than when we have none. Such was the case for a friend of mine and her husband. They had been married thirteen years, had been as anxious as anyone they knew to have a family, but this was not their blessing. However, in time, their long-held hopes were realized. She was to give birth to a baby!

All was joy. Pregnancy did not agree with her; she was sick for the entire time. The baby seemed to be all right, but the mother, at the time of delivery, weighed one-half pound less than she had in the beginning—nine months before. The sickness of those months was soon forgotten in their happiness at having a little girl of their own. They were not able to have more children, but they did have one. Their family now seemed complete; they could ask no more.

The child grew and so also did their happiness. Then there was a terrible accident, and their beloved daughter was killed.

I don't know if this sister understood the role of Eve—and

thereby of woman—to nurture those around her, but she did find her solace in just this way. It was not long after the passing of her daughter that her husband was called to serve as a mission president. The two of them very soon found themselves surrounded by nearly two hundred young people and mature couples. Many of them needed help. Some were homesick, or discouraged, or both. Occasionally one was physically ill; some were so overwhelmed by the challenges of mission life that they thought they couldn't go on. (She understood that feeling very well.) There was need of someone to encourage them, to inspire them, to show them they were cared about. She, of course, was one who might do this—but could she?

She found, at first with effort, that she could and she did. With attention and caring the missionaries responded; they could go on. She found that she too had the courage she needed to succeed in her mission. She was helping, nurturing, "mothering" the missionaries, she thought, but it was for herself, too, that she cared. Then she went beyond the missionaries and was making friends for the mission. She felt an abundance of love.

This giving of self to others is as old as Eve, and the happiness that accompanies it she knew too. Teachers know this, nurses know it, neighbors too. Because of woman's assignment by the Lord to nurture and care for all living, she will, by nature, find fulfillment in nurturing those who need a caring heart or sincere concern.

My husband and I once traveled abroad to visit our daughter, who was living and serving in London with her husband, the president of the England London Mission. In this beautiful and historic city we enjoyed seeing many architectural attractions, great triumphs of steel and stone. But more than these, we were drawn to the missionaries, each one looking just like the next, yet no two really alike. We loved seeing them; whether two by two or in a group, their crisp appearance called attention to them and the gospel light radiant in their eyes labeled them missionaries as clearly as the name badges they wore. The sisters—lovely, hair gleaming, faces beaming—you knew they had a story to tell if only you'd just listen.

Having worked so much with the women, I thought of mothers at home praying for these missionaries, pleading for their success. We were stimulated by their zone meetings and touched by their testimonies. Their everyday talk had a charm that found us sometimes asking them to explain unusual expressions.

One of these phrases, while not unique to London, does still remind us of those special missionaries and their labors in that city. The expression, *mind the gap,* I remember as I remember them, however, not for the meaning it had to them, but for what it can mean to each of us. In the city it is posted on the walls of the Underground. As you may already know, when the train comes into the station and the automatic doors slide open, ideally the floor of the car meets the platform in a way for passengers to easily walk in and out of the train. However, there can be a fairly wide space between the station platform and floor of the car—a *gap.* One young missionary explained how easy it is, when you are concerned about other things, to forget about that space; you could get your foot wedged in the gap. The city, to absolve itself of any culpability should someone put a foot in that space or even drop something into the hole, shifts responsibility for any risk to the riders by a loudspeaker telling them to look out for possible problems, or *mind the gap*.

We did not travel by the Underground as much as the missionaries, so we did not have difficulties with those particular gaps, but I have thought about that warning and how appropriate it is for our lives.

We can find little about Eve's life from the time she was working in the field with Adam. We don't know what goals she may have had or how she achieved, but I do know for myself and the women I have known best through my lifetime that we had hopes and goals to achieve them. We talked about what we wanted to "be" when we grew up. We made plans and lists. There were things like learning to tap dance and playing the piano and singing and becoming a teacher— the high-minded or serious and casual or even flippant all together. Some were dropped from the list without much notice as our tastes and judgments matured. But there were many serious goals, some that we didn't make with our friends but that were the result of our looking around us at the lives of people we admired, and most of all, the result of prayer. These we kept and refined and worked on and continued to pray about. We wanted these to happen. Usually those about which we were prayerful and serious did happen. Partly this was because we lived for those things and observed the requirements. We did what it took to bridge the distance from where we were to where we wanted to be. We minded the gap.

If we have used an everyday expression known best by a workaday world in some other place to express a serious concept, we have done this in order to think freshly about an idea that isn't new. Setting and reaching for a goal is not a new idea, but this is a new time in our lives.

Let it be a time to sort and select, keeping the habits that have helped, but by all means eliminating and starting afresh where something needs to be better. Coming to one's fiftieth year or beyond is an important time—not the kind of important that needs a party with others, but clearly a time for personal prayer and projecting toward the years ahead. If we should fail to mind the gap, and get our foot stuck in the space between, it will be hard to move ahead and to get where we'd like to be. Let's try to avoid the "That's just the way I am" stance, unless it is also just the way we want to be.

The story of Mother Eve is like a gift of the Lord to each woman who will take the time to find in it the almost hidden treasures it contains. We surely did not mine it all. I really believe this story has been given as a model for each of us as women, to learn about who we really are—our need to love and to serve, to pray and to obey and keep the Lord's commandments. The unrecorded period of Eve's life, from the time she helped Adam in the field until she gained her crown of righteousness, is for us to fill in with our own lives. And the best thing about this story is that it is true, you know.

## *Note*

Barbara B. Smith was general Relief Society president from 1974 to 1984. She has served on Utah's sesquicentennial committee, the national board of American Mother, Inc., Governor Michael Leavitt's GIFT committee for the advancement of families, and many other associations. She is married to Douglas H. Smith, and they have seven children, thirty-nine grandchildren, and fifteen great-grandchildren.

# Index